Problems in Roofing Design

Problems in Roofing Design

B. Harrison McCampbell, AIA

Butterworth Architecture
Boston   London   Oxford   Singapore   Sydney   Toronto   Wellington

Butterworth Architecture is an imprint of Butterworth–Heinemann
Copyright © 1991 by Butterworth–Heinemann, a division of Reed Publishing (USA) Inc.
All rights reserved.

 Recognizing the importance of preserving what has been written, it is the policy of
Butterworth–Heinemann to have the books it publishes printed on acid-free paper, and
we exert our best efforts to that end.

Library of Congress Cataloging-in-Publication Data
McCampbell, B. Harrison.
       Problems in roofing design / B. Harrison McCampbell.
           p.   cm.
       ISBN 0-7506-9162-X (alk. paper)
       1. Roofs—Design and construction.   I. Title.
       TH2401.M37 1992   91–29945
       695—dc20   CIP

British Library Cataloguing in Publication Data
McCampbell, B. Harrison
       Problems in roofing design.
       I. Title
       695

       ISBN 0-7506-9162-X

Butterworth–Heinemann
80 Montvale Avenue
Stoneham, MA 02180

10 9 8 7 6 5 4 3 2 1

Printed in the United States of America

Dedication

I would like to dedicate this book to my parents,
Joseph Samuel and Marguerite Harrison McCampbell
who found time to rear eight children and teach us all
to do what is right.

Contents

Preface

How many times during the course of discussion with other design professionals, either from within your firm or one of your competitors' firms, have you heard, "Oh, I don't ever draw any roofing details. I don't want to accept the responsibility if it leaks." Or, "I'm not sure what the best flashing method is. I'll let the roofer figure it out—that's his job!"

These statements are most likely the prelude to a roofing failure. If not a total failure, at least a roof that fails to keep the water out successfully. Architects, through fear or ignorance, have sometimes taken the "head in the sand" approach when it comes to telling the contractor how to construct the building. From a contractor's point of view, he does not want to assume a designer's responsiblity. But that is exactly what he does if he builds something without a detail that has been incorporated as part of the project documents. Even if a detail is not provided in the drawings, a sketch can be made in the field during construction that illustrates how a specific condition is to be built, and then added to the record set as an integral part of the contract.

This book is written to point out to architects the need for them to take control of, and responsibility for, their design so as to ensure they get what they want. This assumes, of course, that they know exactly what it is they want and know how to go about getting it.

This is meant to act as a reference book that can be studied in general or used as a guideline in the production of the working drawings. More than likely, most of the details created on your next project will not be found among those illustrated in this book, but the moisture control philosophy used throughout will hopefully guide the designer in the right direction. This book is also not meant to be a sole source of information concerning roofing details, but rather to point up how the details in the NRCA and SMACNA manuals are to be incorporated into your working drawings.

Take the time to coordinate the details with the plans and sections throughout the rest of the drawings, producing a clear, concise, graphic representation of what will someday be a performing roofing system. And if you don't know how a detail is supposed to work—Ask! Don't just think about it and not detail it, assuming the installer is thinking the same thing. Louis Kahn once said "Sometimes you think you're thinking, but you're not. And that usually occurs when you're not drawing!"

Acknowledgments

I would like to thank the following people who have contributed in one way or another toward the production of this book:

Mr. Richard P. Baxter

Mr. Richard E. Fricklas

Mr. William F. Martin

Mr. Kenneth G. Schneider

Mr. Peter van Dijk

Introduction

It has been reported that money spent on installing the roof on a new building amounts to less than 5% of the total cost of that building. It has also been reported that whenever construction lawsuits are instigated, that roofing problems are the cause of 60% to 80% of the millions of dollars spent on litigation and settlement. Hundreds of building owners and homeowner's associations across the United States are plantiffs against developers, builders, architects, contractors, and subcontractors because their buildings leak, crack, move, and simply fall apart due to shoddy design and construction. Of course, each case has its own set of problems and responsible parties, but in almost every case the building team—those with any involvement in the design and/or construction of the project—is called into civil litigation proceedings to defend itself.

One contributory problem is the fact that a number of architects rely on the building codes to provide protection against faulty construction. But in reading the first page of the Uniform Building Code, it states that "The purpose of this code is to provide minimum standards to safeguard life or limb, health, property and public welfare...." If it is a minimum set of standards and the architect refers to anything he might not have covered in his project documents as "...or as per local building code," the project is being constructed to last for a minimum number of years with no room for error. A minimum standard means just what it says—that this is the least that a building needs to be safe for habitation.

Along with that, it would seem the building code congress assumes a certain level of competency with the building trades. But in the larger cities, where the labor pool is plentiful but sometimes undertrained, craftsmanship is sometimes learned on the job by a laborer who, in many cases, is working his first job. Thus, the builder is able to compete in a fiercely competitive market with inexpensive labor.

The nature of construction is such, however, that mistakes can easily be covered up and may or may not be discovered until a much later date. By this time, the latest owner may have inherited problems that, had he or she known of them at the time the building was being purchased, could have prompted him to negotiate a lower price or back out of the deal altogether.

Where an architect can extend his or her protection in this scenario is to learn as much as possible about good construction while learning about good design. The colleges and universities are already at odds to teach the architect-to-be in a five-year program all that is basically necessary to go out into the world and blossom into a practicing architect. But, along the way, the theory of school does not leave much time for the practicality of survival in an increasingly competitive world. Architects are being asked to first design a building and then to tell the general contractor how to put it together through a set of drawings and specifications. It seems like an impossible task to expect an architect to detail how a building is to be put together so that it won't leak, move, or crack. But in the construction process, the architect designs the building, and the general contractor builds it the way the architect tells him to. The contractors in the field are not there to design as they go if the documents do not supply them with sufficient information. They are to be told what and how to build, and they build it.

With the advent of America's increasing reliance on the judicial process to solve problems, the architect is in a small party of people in comparison with the numbers he or she is potentially up against. There are approximately 60,000 registered architects in a country of over 230,000,000 people. So the power one exerts in defending oneself in a court of law has to come with the greatest efficiency—and that is to use as many tools as possible to protect oneself against the liabilities of the profession. One of the best ways comes from the old adage, "An ounce of prevention is worth a pound of cure."

This leads to the driving force behind the publication of this book. As an architect who has been involved with the roofing industry since 1977, I have found that the majority of the time a roof leaks, it is due to problems associated with the edges and penetrations. Any place the roof changes planes or direction, there is almost always a chance that a leak will occur. Normally the field of the roof is installed without much trouble. But the greatest amount of care should go into the areas most needing attention—the sheet metal, the flashing, and the methods of field termination, which are attended to in the roofing details.

No matter what kind of roofing system is used, most of the basic guidelines are alike: the field of the roof is terminated in some fashion with mechanical fasteners that almost always penetrate the roof membrane, and those penetrations have to be covered, or flashed, with a material usually thicker than, and compatible with, the field membrane.

The problems in this book refer mainly to asphalt built-up roofing. But by no means is this to cast any aspersions on the built-up roofing industry. It just happens that while living in Southern California, the majority of the roofing I encounter is built up. The problems result from faulty design or could have been at least minimized, if not avoided entirely, had the designer supplied the contractor with a detail showing exactly what was to have been done.

No matter what kind of roofing system is used, refer to either the manufacturer's details or the National Roofing Contractors Association (NRCA) manual to get an idea of how the termination and flashing is done and apply that method to the individual details that need specific attention on your particular project. Use the assistance of a manufacturer's representative, an independent roofing consultant, or a qualified roofing contractor to see that proper attention is paid to the roof and its details during the design phase. "Walk through" the roof construction and visualize how walls come together, how edges will look and work from both above and below, and how penetrations affect the roofing field. By providing ample details, the bidders get a better idea of how much time and materials will be needed to install the roof, and surprises, in the form of added costs, will be kept to a minimum. Once a job is bid and awarded, adds will be much more costly to the project than if they were addressed during the drawing phase.

It only seems rational that the architect would want to spend an additional $1,000 in the production of another page or two of roofing-related details and minimize the amount of liability on the front end of a building's construction. Whereas, on the other end, if these problems are caused by a lack of details and direction, $1,000 will not begin to cover the cost of either extra change orders or litigation proceedings.

 As a general rule, one should refer to both the NRCA handbook and the Sheet Metal and Air-Conditioning Contractors' National Association (SMACNA) manual for general information about roofing and sheet metal. Since it is virtually impossible to present every conceivable detail in these two publications, this book will take problems experienced in existing construction projects and show how they could have perhaps been avoided by presenting the general contractor or the roofing contractor with an appropriate detail in the construction documents. In most cases, the drawings or specifications did not address the problems experienced, and the resulting installation was left to the installing contractor's field laborers.

So, again, just because this book refers mainly to built-up roofing and your office perhaps specifies only single-ply roofing systems, don't limit your scope of learning by getting hung up on the system. This book is meant to teach the philosophy of good roofing design. Learn methods that will apply to any type of roofing materials used so that water entry is controlled from the office through good design rather than taking the chance that it is achieved in the field. The latter puts your fate as a successful architect in the builder's hands, and not yours. What is a building, and its designer, really worth if the pleasant visual aspects and daily function are upset by water intrusion in the form of wet floors and stained walls and ceilings?

Another point of discussion is the method of substrate construction. Whether or not the decking material shown is germane to what is used in your area, be it plywood, steel, or concrete, consult your structural engineer to ensure that the proper methods and materials that your individual project requires are used.

Rules of Good Roofing Practice

There are a few general rules of good roofing practice that should be adhered to during the design phase:

- The first step toward having a successful roof is to have good positive drainage. Build the slope into the roof through the incline of the substrate at a rate of at least 1/4" per foot. One-half inch should be enough on the high side for most low-sloped roofs. Anything steeper than that will take extra care in the selection of materials and methods of installation, so beware.

- Keep roof drains away from column lines. It is always convenient to hide downspout piping within the web of a steel column, but,unfortunately, the top of the column is at the high point of the roof. The best location for the roof drain is at mid-span of the structural member where the low point is, or along an exterior wall with the structure sloping down toward the wall. Then you could use "crickets" or "saddles" to divert the water in a positive fashion along the walls to each roof drain.

- Try to avoid using gravel on your roofs. Gravel, if not already, is soon to be a limited-quantity item. There is only so much. Not unlike water, it has always been around. But everything has a limit. Smooth-surface roofs are lighter in weight and easier to maintain. If you use a coating on the roof, that also serves two purposes—it eases the thermal load on the immediate roof surface and it allows the maintenance to be generally limited to the coating and not the roofing material below.

- Use a flexible flashing material. That is where movement occurs.Almost every manufacturer now offers some type of material that allows for more movement than the field material. Utilize it. And when specifying the wall flashing for built-up roofs, make sure to call for the sheet flashing material used on a wall 24" or higher to be "strapped." This means that the flashing is to be installed in a vertical fashion, no more than 36" wide. This keeps the roofer from using long horizontal applications that usually sag due to the inability of the material to support itself. It is also due to the fact that too large a piece of flashing allows the asphalt to cool prior to installation, resulting in a condition where the flashing is not fully adhered to the wall, causing blistering. The material can be installed in a horizontal fashion on walls under 24" in height , but make sure to specify a maximum flashing length of 10'-0" to keep the asphalt hot for proper adhesion.

- Use lead boots and caps on vent pipes. Keep roof maintenance down.

- Specify cast iron assemblies on roof drains. PVC will not last as long. The amount of money spent over the life of a roof drain for cast iron is limited, whereas the amount spent in constantly replacing anything else is not.

- Provide at least a 4" flange on gravel stop and pitch pocket sheet metal (minimun 24 gauge). This allows ample space to cover the fasteners properly.

- Don't hesitate to use gutters. Control water when possible.

- Keep curb and counterflashing heights at an 8" minimum.

- Keep a minimum of 18" between curbs, pipes, and edges of the roof.

- Roofing should be watertight without counterflashing. Seal the top edge of flashing material, especially if the metal counterflashing above is surface mounted.

- Whenever possible, specify that the roofing material is installed prior to the installation of the curbs, whether factory-installed or field-fabricated. This way the curb is "sandwiched" in roofing material. Nonetheless, consult the manufacturer's recommendations.

- Try to change the shape of a roof penetration to avoid the use of a pitch pocket. But if you must use a pitch pocket, keep the size down o where the outer edge of the pitch pocket is 2" from the outer edges of the roof penetration. Too much mastic will only become a maintenance headache.

- Don't rely on manufacturer's recommendations from one printed sheet to supply your job with all necessary information pertaining to your particular design. The architect may believe that the manufacturer shows and controls all details to protect itself. That is why you have to take control yourself and ask questions of your selected manufacturer or an independent roofing consultant as you design. It will involve them early on and could possibly save money in the long run.

- As you are designing the roof on your next new building, keep in mind that the roofing system will need maintenance, repair, and eventually, replacement. Don't design-in problems that can save you money now but cost you money down the road, as in low curb and counterflashing heights, thin one-piece counterflashing that is worthless once it is turned up, and so on.

- Finally, pay attention to the sheet metal details. Most of the time, the sheet metal gets neglected, yet it carries a great amount of responsibility. Almost always, sheet metal is called out to terminate and/or counterflash a roofing material. So don't try to save money on such a critical area, and don't be afraid to call for a thicker minimum than that required by code. Remember, the code is simply saying that, for example, 26 gauge is the least amount of thickness needed for the job. In some situations, that may not be enough.

Problems in Roofing Design

PART I

Problems and Recommendations

This section points out anomalies encountered during inspections of existing roofs that could have been avoided if addressed in the working drawings. The photograph shows the problem observed, the sketch shows a possible solution, and the text describes both, along with a general "rule of thumb."

Fasteners are backing out of coping

Observation Fasteners used to secure metal coping are showing signs of movement and are beginning to pull out. Metal coping expands and contracts at a different rate than the wood nailer it is installed on, causing differential movement in the shaft of the fastener. Cyclic action will eventually work the head of the nail back and forth until it extricates itself from the wood nailer below.

An added detriment to nailing on the horizontal is that when the hammer pounds the nail head into the metal coping,a small concave area almost always surrounds the nail head. This causes a small ponding condition right at the point of penetration.

Recommendation Fasten metal coping only on the inside vertical face using screw-type fasteners with a neoprene washer head. If the screw is to ever work its way out, water has little chance of entering the wall's waterproofing system. Using the vertical face for fastening eliminates the chance of standing water at the fastener.

Design Principle Fasten metal coping only on vertical surfaces.

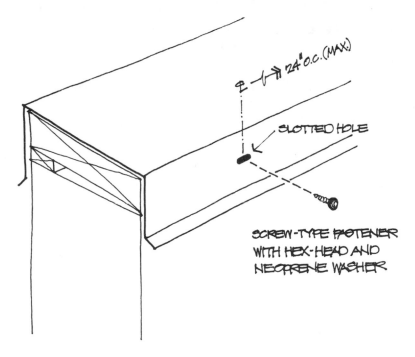

¢ —⊢→ 24" O.C. (MAX.)

SLOTTED HOLE

SCREW-TYPE FASTENER
WITH HEX-HEAD AND
NEOPRENE WASHER

Odd-shaped wall is hard to flash

Observation Widening of a wall makes for a strange sheet metal configuration, consequently causing differential movement along joints. As presently constructed, joints in the sheet metal coping will always be a maintenance item, requiring constant vigilance and repair. Caulking cannot be expected to withstand moisture attack on a regular basis. Expensive, high-quality caulking works better than cheaper, low-grade caulking, but still will not last forever.

Recommendation Using a standing-seam joint method, keep the number of seams to a minimum, making water entry less likely to happen. Joints should be provided along any point in the coping where the profile changes directions or at 10'-0" maximum, the longest length of most sheet metal.

Design Principle Don't leave design decisions to field personnel.

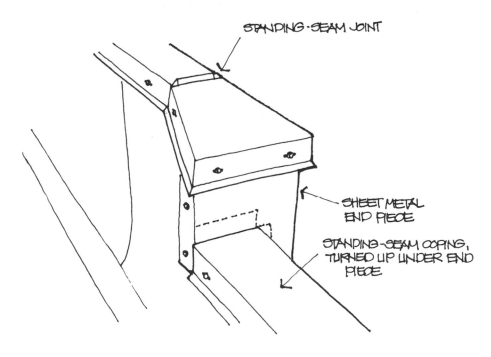

STANDING-SEAM JOINT

SHEET METAL
END PIECE

STANDING-SEAM COPING,
TURNED UP UNDER END
PIECE

Wall is open at end of coping

Observation   Metal coping terminates into precast concrete cornice without adequate connection and allowance for expansion and contraction. Caulking cannot be expected to carry the load for both movement and keeping out possible water entry.

Recommendation   Custom-made sheet metal end piece should be affixed to precast cornice and designed with a four-ply flat-lock seam. The flange of the end piece should be set in caulking and fastened with washer-head screws. Ideally, the best condition for flashing's sake would be to have the metal coping abutting the cornice at least 3" below the top of the cornice. Then the flange would be mounted on the vertical surface and not on the horizontal as is now the case for a repair attempt.

Design Principle   Don't leave design decisions to field personnel.

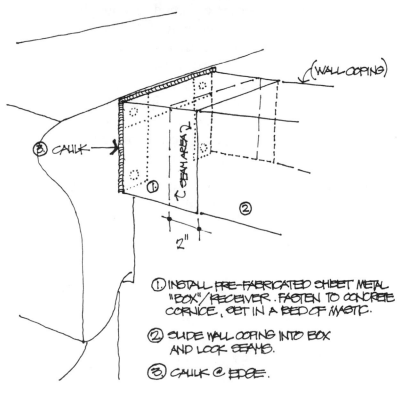

(WALL COPING)

③ CAULK →

SEAM AREA

① ②

2"

① INSTALL PRE-FABRICATED SHEET METAL "BOX"/RECEIVER. FASTEN TO CONCRETE CORNICE, SET IN A BED OF MASTIC.

② SLIDE WALL COPING INTO BOX AND LOCK SEAMS.

③ CAULK @ EDGE.

Algae is visible on metal coping

Observation Discoloration on top of the coping has resulted from constant ponding of water. The coping was installed without any positive slope. Therefore, any prolonged moisture, even from an overnight fog, will stand on, and cause deterioration of, the painted finish of the metal coping.

Recommendation Remove the coping and re-install same with wood shims designed to slope the coping toward the interior at 1" in 12". This will not only prevent any further discoloration, but will minimize the chance of possible water intrusion at the joints. A standing-seam or flat-lock seam would have helped in this instance, but simply sloping the coping can have a more advantageous effect, no matter what seaming method is used.

Design Principle Specify metal coping to have positive slope toward the interior.

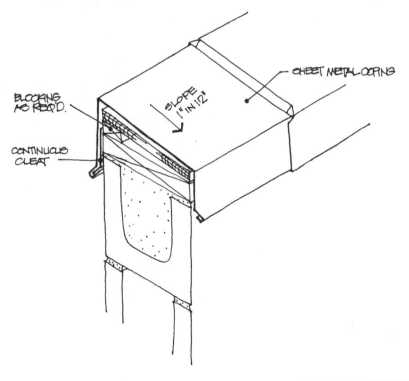

CHEET METAL COPING

SLOPE 1" IN 12"

BLOCKING AS REQ'D.

CONTINUOUS CLEAT

5

Water stains are visible at joint in coping

Observation Stain marks below the sheet metal coping were occurring most consistently at the location of the joints. Overall, the coping was not sloped back toward the interior (roof side), but was installed flat. Ponding was greatest along the central axis of the coping, and, because the joints were a simple lap-joint with caulking, they consequently failed, allowing water to enter at almost every joint. This constant presence of water in a porous material such as stucco, is a veritable breeding ground for algae and fungus.

Recommendation Re-install the coping, using either a cover plate over the existing metal joints, or fabricate new metal coping using standing-seams or flat-lock seams. Whichever direction taken should follow the most basic rule against water entry: Incorporate positive drainage by sloping the coping at least 1" in 12" toward the inside.

Extra blocking is best utilized underneath the 2" thick wood nailer so that the top face of the nailer can fully support the coping, especially if the joint of the sheet metal is only lapped 2" to 4" and caulked.

Design Principle Slope metal coping toward the interior of the building.

SLOPE 1:12 TO INTERIOR

← FASTEN @ 24" O.C.

(OUTSIDE)   (INSIDE)

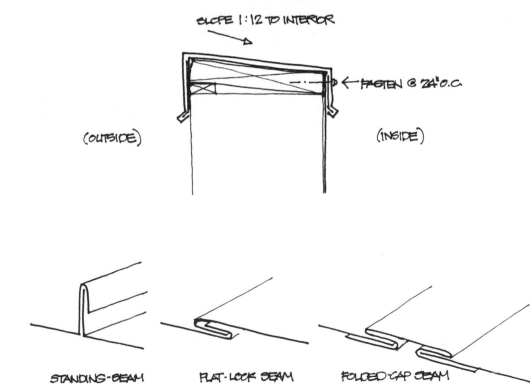

STANDING-SEAM   FLAT-LOCK SEAM   FOLDED-CAP SEAM

6

Coping was installed too low to roof

Observation Sheet metal coping has been installed atop a short parapet wall that is so close to the roofing surface that any wind-driven ponded water has a tendency to lap up over the base flashing and enter the building's interior at the wall.

For a wall this short, a coping is not the right choice unless the height of the wall is raised or the level of the roof is dropped, depending on the design criteria. The minimum height of a parapet should be 8".

Recommendation If the wall height and the roof level, as in this case, are fixed and necessary for the design's success, the coping should be deleted. In its place, a gravel stop and tapered insulation assembly should be used as a way to achieve the desired exterior fascia profile, while lifting the perimeter fastening and flashing up and out of the threat of possible water intrusion.

Either a multiple layer of tapered insulation or a tapered edge transition built into the roof deck is what is required to allow the built-up roofing membrane to bridge the height difference between the roof level and the top of the exterior wall.

Design Principle All curb and parapet heights should be at least 8".

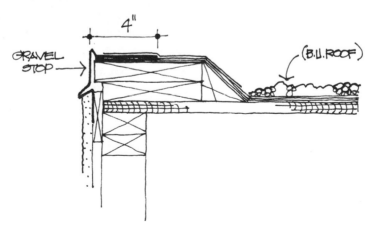

Metal coping was not properly fastened

Observation The inside corner of a perimeter parapet wall had its metal coping displaced during a recent light windstorm. The wind was mild enough that it simply blew the coping up and dropped it back into place. But investigation showed that the only fastening for the coping on the entire roof was done at the standing-seam joints, at 10'-0" on center. The bottom piece of metal coping was fastened to the substrate, and the next piece was hooked into the lip of the first, actually not mechanically fastened but on one end. When a corner came up, the sheet metal installer simply continued the inside at the turn and used the piece cut out at the corner to make the standing-seam joint.

Recommendation This coping should have been designed with a continuous metal clip along the outside edge as the fastening device for wind protection. The inside face could then be secured by a screw-type fastener with a neoprene washer-head holding down the inside face, using 24" center-to-center fastening. This makes for easy removal during repairs and re-roofing at a later date, thereby allowing the coping to be reused.

Design Principle Secure metal coping with a continuous clip along the outside face and fasteners along the inside face.

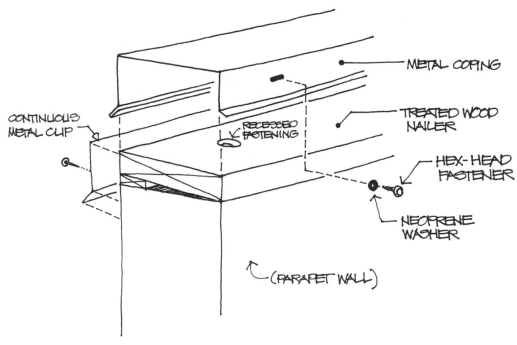

CONTINUOUS METAL CLIP

RECESSED FASTENING

METAL COPING

TREATED WOOD NAILER

HEX-HEAD FASTENER

NEOPRENE WASHER

(PARAPET WALL)

8

Metal coping leaks at junction

Observation An area on the perimeter of a roof, where various levels of coping came together, had been a contributor to numerous maintenance repairs after leaks had been reported below. In the past, a supplementary wall had been added at the location of a step-down on the original roof's parapet wall and made the tie-in difficult. Many corners were open and hard to repair due to the expansion and contraction of the sheet metal.

Recommendation When the secondary wall coping was added, the designer should have built up the wall so that a smooth, planar surface, though varying in width, could have been the setting for the metal coping. Then a standing-seam or a flat-lock seam could easily make the transition in width when the coping needed to do so. It is also at that time the nailer for the coping can be specified as sloping at least 1/2" in 12" to ensure that there will be no standing water on the coping, and water can safely fall onto the roof.

Design Principle Keep details simple so that construction is simple.

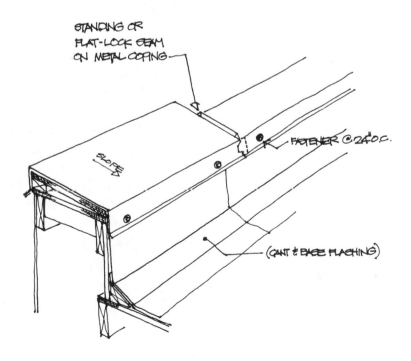

STANDING OR
FLAT-LOCK SEAM
ON METAL COPING

SLOPE

FASTENER @ 24" O.C.

(CANT & BASE FLASHING)

Metal coping has blown off wall

Observation A metal coping had been installed along the top of a mansard roof that was constructed of clay tile on a sloping face. Winds had blown up hard enough one day to travel up the tile and lift up a rather long leg of the coping that had been designed simply to cover the fasteners holding down the top row of tiles. It was discovered that the wide section of metal itself was not secured, and that the only mechanical fastening in the coping at all was down through the top of the wall in a somewhat sporadic pattern. The wind then lifted the metal up in most cases and all the way off in others.

Recommendation The metal used had only been as thick as required by the Uniform Building Code—26 gauge. In this case, however, thicker metal was required to properly withstand the forces created by both the wind and the shape of the roof's design. As was the case, the valleys of the clay tile became small wind tunnels that dead-ended in the pocket created by the wall and the sheet metal. So the metal in this instance was the point of least resistance and bent up when the wind velocity increased.

Design Principle Design materials as the conditions demand, not as the building code allows.

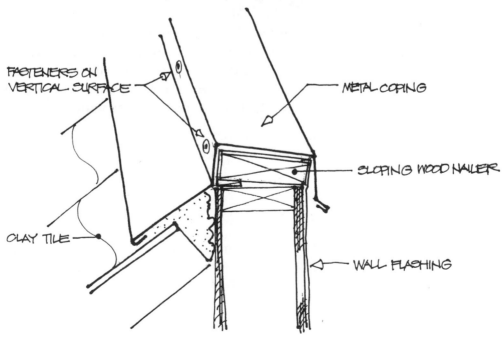

FASTENERS ON VERTICAL SURFACE

METAL COPING

SLOPING WOOD NAILER

CLAY TILE

WALL FLASHING

10

Wood nailer is exposed below coping

Observation   Leaks were discovered all along a wall that was capped with a metal coping. However, the metal coping was not even deep enough to cover the nailer that it was fastened to, thereby allowing water to drip along the edge of a flat face and enter the wall behind the stucco.

Recommendation   The metal coping should always extend at least 1" below the bottom edge of the nailer below it to ensure against any water blowing up the face of a parapet wall and into the wall's interior. This applies to the inside and outside faces of the metal. Also each face should have at least a 1/2" fold in the bottom edge that turns out at least 30° away from the building face to create a drip edge. On the outside face, this fold is the hook strip that goes over a metal cleat or clip that may or may not be continuous along the wall, also fastened into the nailer.

Design Principle   Ensure that all points of possible water entry are amply protected.

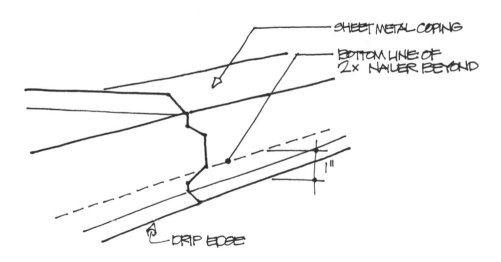

SHEET METAL COPING

BOTTOM LINE OF
2× NAILER BEYOND

1"

DRIP EDGE

Flood coat and gravel are running off roof

Observation The asphalt flood coat, along with roofing gravel, is migrating down the face of a shingle roof. Edging along the built-up roofing has not been properly terminated during design and/or construction. Built-up roofing bitumen and gravel need to be separated from dissimilar roofing materials with sheet metal.

Recommendations A sheet metal gravel stop should be installed under the edge of the built-up roofing with a minimum 4" flange, and the bottom flange extending down a minimum of 4" over the top of the shingle face below. Slots or holes could be added to the vertical flange to allow for free flow of water, if desired. The sheet metal should also be folded along the bottom edge to ensure the metal will have a straight line.

Design Principle Be aware of the limitations of all roofing materials.

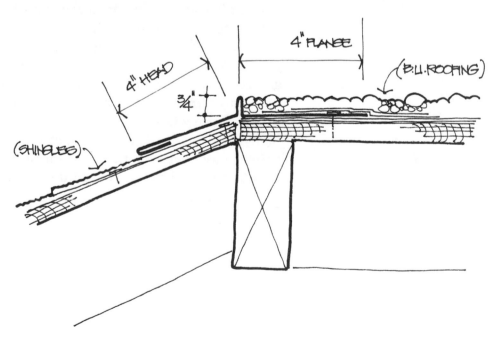

Gravel stop is open at junction

Observation Metal gravel stop is not terminated properly at the juncture of built-up roofing and a shingle roof. The opening in the roof will be a constant item for maintenance personnel to repair. Water entry will always be not only a possibility, but an ever-present threat, due to the differential movement in the sheet metal gravel stop, the shingles, the built-up roof, and the wood below all of these.

Recommendation Continue the sheet metal gravel stop in a straight line across the top of the shingles, extending the built-up roofing out to the edge of the existing built-up roofing. Design the gravel guard height to be high enough to keep the gravel on the roof, but low enough to allow the water to drain without excessive ponding. Proper flange width (4") allows the metal to be nailed in a staggered pattern and still allow enough room between the nail nearest the outside edge and the gravel guard itself to be flashed adequately.

Design Principle Don't leave design decisions to field personnel.

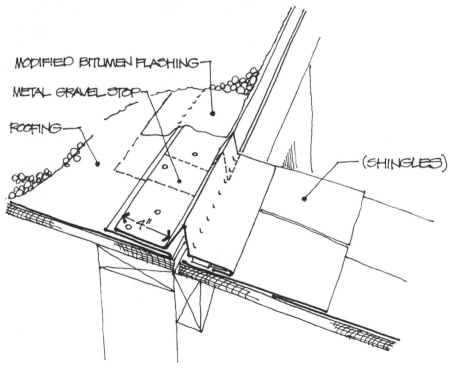

MODIFIED BITUMEN FLASHING

METAL GRAVEL STOP

ROOFING

4"

(SHINGLES)

Nail in gravel stop is too close to edge

Observation   Roofing material was discovered to be delaminating all along a gravel stop, apparently originating at the locations of the nails used to secure the metal edging. Besides backing out, the nails were pushing up the protective flashing and rusting, thereby creating leaks at the edge.

Recommendation   Specify that the nails holding the gravel stop in place be kept back from the outer edge at least 1½" so that the flashing material has ample room to adhere to the metal between the nail and the outer lip of the gravel stop. This must be prefaced, however, by also specifying that the gravel stop flange be 4" in width. Any shorter and you cannot stagger the nails properly, something that needs to be done to reduce wind uplift. Flanges wider than 4" are a waste of material. Also specify that the treated wood nailer below the gravel stop is at least as wide as the flange, preferably wider, so that the metal has a sufficient base on which to perform and be fastened into.

The cleat, if required, can easily be fastened into the face of the nailer and make for a uniform, secure termination of the roofing material.

Design Principle   Design and detail typical roofing terminations that can be used from one job to the next. Don't assume the roofing applicators have your best interests in mind.

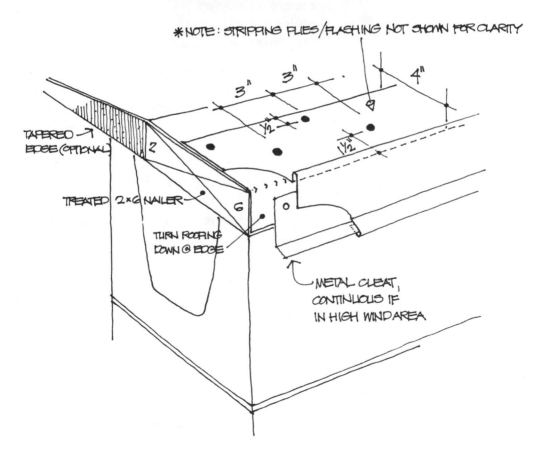

* NOTE: STRIPPING PLIES/FLASHING NOT SHOWN FOR CLARITY

3" 3" 4"

TAPERED
EDGE (OPTIONAL)

½"

1½"

TREATED 2×6 NAILER

TURN ROOFING
DOWN @ EDGE

METAL CLEAT,
CONTINUOUS IF
IN HIGH WIND AREA

Gravel stop is not stabilized

Observation During a roof inspection, it was discovered that a single-ply roofing system had been attached to a metal gravel stop that itself had not been fastened into the structural substrate. The roofing material had contracted with time and had begun to pull in around the edges. So since the gravel stop metal had not been anchored, it pulled completely away from the edge, thereby exposing the building to water intrusion.

Recommendation The metal gravel stop should be properly secured against any movement in order to protect the edge termination of the roofing system. Make the flange at least 4″ wide and stagger the nails so that the gravel stop has enough resistance to forces pulling it from the inside and pushing it up from the outside, in the case of high winds. And in high wind areas, a continuous metal clip of at least 20-gauge metal should be incorporated into the edge detail.

Design Principle Make sure that the edge of the roof and its accessories are properly secured and watertight.

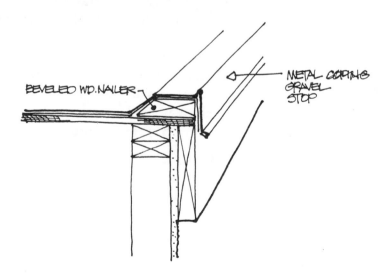

BEVELED WD. NAILER

METAL COPING
GRAVEL
STOP

Counterflashing is pulling away from chimney

Observation   Metal counterflashing is beginning to open up at the top, allowing possible water entry into roofing system below. The counterflashing is not properly mounted to chimney. Fasteners have failed due to PVC roofing material shrinking and pulling the PVC-coated metal away from the masonry. Caulking is nothing more than a temporary seal along the top.

Recommendation   Proper procedure for counterflashing would be to make it in two parts. First, surface-mount a receiver piece onto the existing brick, followed by a separate piece of sheet metal to be wedged into the receiver, allowing possible removal during future re-roofing. Roofing material should be mechanically fastened into the horizontal plane and flashed over, turning the flashing up and terminating it at the top, under the new counterflashing.

Design Principle   Use surface-mounted counterflashing as a last resort, especially on a rough-texture surface like stucco, brick, or masonry.

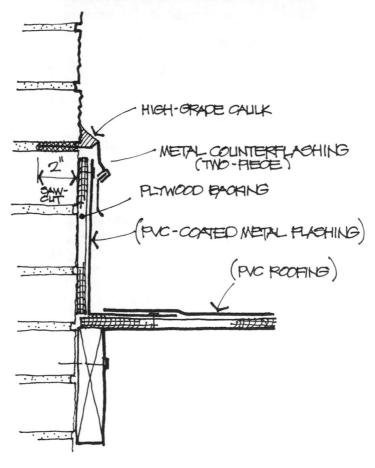

HIGH-GRADE CAULK

METAL COUNTERFLASHING
(TWO-PIECE)

2"

SAW-CUT

PLYWOOD BACKING

(PVC-COATED METAL FLASHING)

(PVC ROOFING)

Metal counterflashing is falling off wall

Observation Sheet metal counterflashing is not properly mounted to wall and has fallen off, having relied on an occasional nail and a thin bead of caulk to keep the wall watertight. The junction of the roofing and the vertical wall surface is now open to almost certain water entry.

Recommendation When the wall was being constructed, a two-piece metal counterflashing system should have been installed at least one full block course (8") above the highest point of the roof where it intersects the wall.

If the wall is already built, as in re-roofing this present condition, a surface-mounted reglet could be used, but only if the new metal is set in a continuous bead of caulk, is fastened with neoprene washers on the head of each fastener, and a continuous bead of high-grade caulk is used along the top of the reglet once it is installed.

Design Principle Specify two-piece through-wall counterflashing.

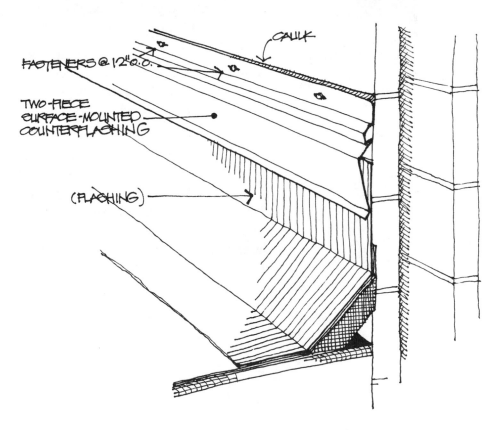

FASTENERS @ 12" O.C.

CAULK

TWO-PIECE
SURFACE-MOUNTED
COUNTERFLASHING

(FLASHING)

Counterflashing is interrupted
by drain pipes

Observation Outlet pipes for a roof drain and its auxiliary drain, both from a roof area located above, exit the common wall through the cast-in-place sheet metal counterflashing. This will be a constant maintenance problem, being that it is impossible to properly flash the sheet metal the way it is now installed. Caulking is the only answer, and that is not a permanent solution.

Recommendation Specify that the pipes are to come no lower than 4" from the top of the sheet metal counterflashing. This way the stucco contractor has enough room to apply his material and seal the pipes in a proper fashion.

It should be noted here, also, that water draining from one roof to another should always have a splash block to land on, and not the bare roofing surface. The capsheet roofing in this problem photograph will suffer accelerated deterioration due to the extra water washing off the granules, and subsequently attacking the roofing system below.

Design Principle Be aware of other design demands when coordinating plans and specifications.

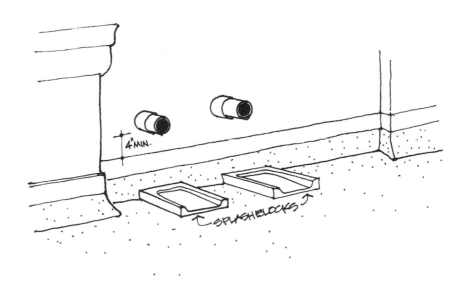

Roof leaks along edge of counterflashing

Observation   Sheet metal counterflashing ends at the edge of the sloping shingle roof section and does not continue, thereby leaving an opening where neither composition shingle nor sheet metal overlap one another.

Recommendation   A piece of custom-made sheet metal should have been designed to cover the intersection where the sloping wall meets the vertical wall. Then a metal edge trim, either fitting over the top of the sloping shingles or under them, should have been installed, followed by the regular metal counterflashing as originally installed, now covering both other flashings below. This way all flashing metal laps "downhill" for proper water runoff.

Design Principle   Design flashing detail at juncture of dissimilar materials.

① INSTALL "L"-SHAPED SHEET METAL
② " " " " EDGE TRIM
③ " " TOP SHEET METAL COUNTERFLASHING
④ " " SHINGLES

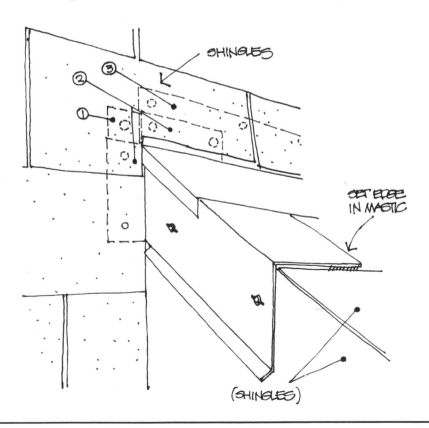

SHINGLES

SET EDGE
IN MASTIC

(SHINGLES)

Counterflashing was installed too low

Observation The sheet metal counterflashing, which doubles as a stucco stop, has been permanently installed as a one-piece counterflashing system. The base flashing for the roof system can go no higher than 5" over the roof level. As tight to the wall as this metal is, it makes access to the flashing below almost impossible, unless the metal is bent up. This is detrimental to the integrity of the metal flashing, though, because it cannot be bent back down to its original shape without the chance of breaking the metal at the radius of the bend.

Recommendation Ideally, a two-piece (removeable) counterflashing should have been specified, with the top of the counterflashing at least 8" over the roof surface, or a minimum of 4" over the top of the cant. This way, whenever the re-roofing process takes place (and it will need re-roofing eventually), the wall flashing can be replaced much easier.

Design Principle Design a roof to be maintained and eventually replaced.

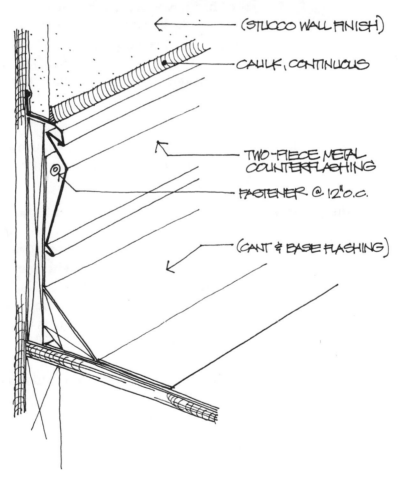

(STUCCO WALL FINISH)

CAULK, CONTINUOUS

TWO-PIECE METAL
COUNTERFLASHING

FASTENER @ 12" O.C.

(CANT & BASE FLASHING)

Leaking discovered along base of chimney

Observation Water was discovered running down the wall below a chimney just after a rather intense rainstorm. On investigation into the integrity of the roofing materials above, it was noted that the chimney was missing the counterflashing along its base and was allowing water entry. Repairs had been attempted with roofing cement, but were not successful. The mastic dried out, cracked, and allowed water to enter as before the repair attempt.

The shingles on the sloped area of the roof just butted into the stucco on the chimney, offering no type of transition, or counterflashing, from one plane to the other.

Recommendation A one-piece sheet metal counterflashing would have been best for this condition, turning up under at least two courses of shingles, and at least 10" up the face of the chimney. The chimney counterflashing height is the most critical due to the fact that water is sheeting down the sloped shingle section and will backwash up against the chimney when it gets to that point. Extra care should be taken in both the design and installation in this case because of the action and reaction of the water during a sudden rainstorm.

Design Principle Control water runoff whenever possible.

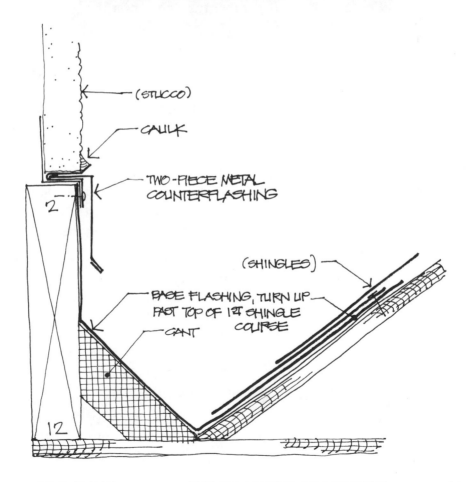

(STUCCO)

CAULK

TWO-PIECE METAL
COUNTERFLASHING

(SHINGLES)

BASE FLASHING, TURN UP
PAST TOP OF 1ST SHINGLE
COURSE

CANT

2

12

Leaking at top of flashing

Observation Leaks were observed as entering a building directly below a firewall that separated two businesses below. There was no termination at the top of the membrane, obviously the most critical area, as this is where water will take the first opportunity to enter the building.

Recommendation In order to eliminate the chance of water entering anywhere along the wall, the most desirable situation would be to encapsulate the wall with flashing material, take it up and over the top of the wall, and install a sheet metal coping along the top over a treated wood nailer.

The next best condition would be to have specified a cast-in-place two-piece metal counterflashing at least 8" above the finished roof so that the counterflashing could be re-moved for maintenance repairs and re-roofing.

The least desirable situation would be to install a two-piece surface-mounted counterflashing. But then you are relying on the caulking along the top of the counterflashing to keep the water out. If this condition is selected, it is best to three-course the top of the wall flashing to protect against possible water entry in case the counterflashing fails.

Design Principle Good roofing practice during the design phase, not caulking during the construction phase, will make and keep a building watertight.

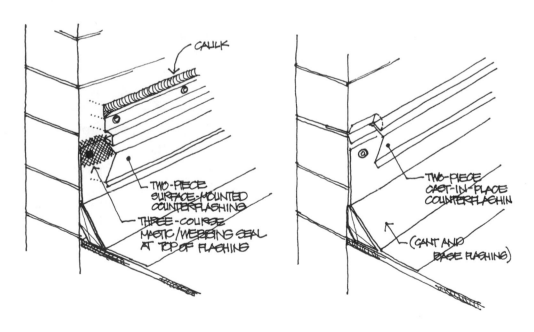

CAULK

TWO-PIECE
SURFACE-MOUNTED
COUNTERFLASHING

THREE-COURSE
MASTIC/WEBBING SEAL
AT TOP OF FLASHING

TWO-PIECE
CAST-IN-PLACE
COUNTERFLASHIN

(CANT AND
BASE FLASHING)

Counterflashing is open at wall intersection

Observation Two walls of differing angles came together above a roof, and their counterflashing was lapped one over the other in a rather awkward fashion, leading to water entry in the building below this detail. Part of the problem was that the stationary, one-piece flashing metal was installed too close to the roofing surface and, during a recent re-roofing process, the metal was bent up to work under. On bending it back down, the metal was not able to return to its original position, consequently leaving an opening.

Recommendation A removable counterflashing system should have been installed originally at least 8" above the finished roofing surface. The stucco is a rather permanent installation and does not allow for a one-piece sheet metal flashing, especially the 24-gauge minimum called for by most codes and architects, to be turned up and down time and again with any measure of success. The two-piece systems on the market nowadays offer enough variation to work with stucco and other materials, and even have pre-fabricated corners, both inside and outside, that will not require the creativity of the sheet metal installer.

Design Principle Design a roof for maintenance and replacement.

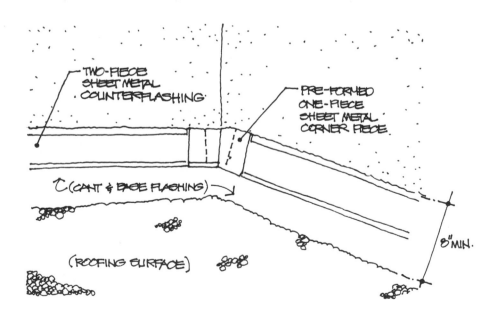

TWO-PIECE SHEET METAL COUNTERFLASHING

PRE-FORMED ONE-PIECE SHEET METAL CORNER PIECE

⌐ (CANT & BASE FLASHING)

(ROOFING SURFACE)

8"MIN.

Gutter is missing at edge

Observation   Water sheeting down the sloping tile roof dead-ends into a low counterflashing condition at the intersection with the adjacent residence.

During heavy rainfall, the cast-in-place counterflashing cannot handle the amount of water being directed its way and allows water intrusion behind the stucco. Also, with the open-ended gutter directing water over the edge and down the stucco wall, stains have resulted, leaving an unsightly discoloration.

Recommendation   Either a one-piece sheet metal gutter or pan should be installed, with the side lining the high wall to be at least 8" higher than the highest point of the gutter or pan. This would then lead out to a downspout in the case of a gutter, or a scupper in the case of a pan, with a splash box of gravel below. The sheet metal should be installed so that the felt underlayment laps the metal edging going up the slope by at least 6" and is sealed with a three-course application of mastic and nylon reinforcement.

Design Principle   Design for maximum storm runoff conditions.

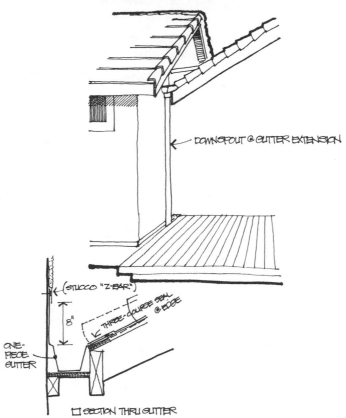

DOWNSPOUT @ GUTTER EXTENSION

(STUCCO "Z-BAR")

THREE-COURSE SEAL @ EDGE

8"

ONE-PIECE GUTTER

◻ SECTION THRU GUTTER

Gutters are filling up with sediment and plants

Observation Plant life was seen growing from a gutter located at the edge of an apartment building. Being an older complex, the trees proximate to the roofs were a constant source of leaves, broken branches, and seeds. Falling anywhere on the roof, these items eventually made it to the low point of the roof, the gutters, by being washed down the slope with each rain. Eventually, without any screens on the gutter or any regular maintenance personnel cleaning them out, the gutters became a long, thin, flower pot and began growing their own bushes and saplings.

Recommendation First of all, the debris needs to be kept out of the gutters as well as possible by screening the material out. This can be accomplished by installing a removeable wire-mesh protection system that will keep out most anything except the fine airborne silt that will filter through even a 1/8" mesh. But, with regular roof maintenance and cleaning out of the gutters twice a year, the plant life can be kept out of the gutters so that they can do what they are designed for—to carry off and control water draining off the roof.

Design Principle Specify roofing components with maintenance in mind.

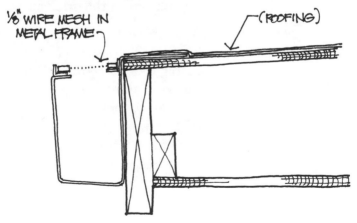

⅛" WIRE MESH IN METAL FRAME

(ROOFING)

Leaking around chimney

Observation Leaks are occurring along the joint between the vertical sheet metal flashing and the adjacent brick. Water entry is also occurring along the top of the flashing at the intersection with the brick.

The sheet metal has been haphazardly installed at the junction between the brick chimney and the capsheet wall flashing. Capsheet flashing has not been terminated properly along the top at the intersection with the brick. Consequently, leaks now occur because the caulking has dried out and has allowed the flashing to separate from the brick surface.

Recommendation Terminate the flashing by either saw-cutting a joint in the masonry for a receiver piece of sheet metal, or surface-mounting a receiver and caulking along the top edge of the new metal. Two-piece metal counterflashing is preferred so that metal can be removed and replaced in future re-roofing and maintenance work. Capsheet flashing should be mechanically fastened along the top at 12" on center, maximum, using cap nails with 1" heads.

Design Principle Design a roof for maintenance and replacement.

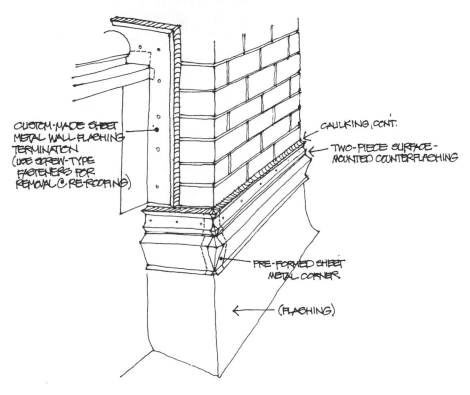

CUSTOM-MADE SHEET
METAL WALL FLASHING
TERMINATION
(USE SCREW-TYPE
FASTENERS FOR
REMOVAL @ RE-ROOFING)

CAULKING, CONT.

TWO-PIECE SURFACE-
MOUNTED COUNTERFLASHING

PRE-FORMED SHEET
METAL CORNER

(FLASHING)

Water is entering building at ledge

Observation   Leaks are occurring at interior of the building below the intersection of the ledge and the vertical wall surface. The ledge is in a direct line with water falling off the tile roof above. The cap sheet roofing has been installed in a one-ply repair along the flat ledge in an attempt at water entry protection.

Recommendation   The ledge should have a sloping sheet metal cap that terminates on the inside under a cast-in-place counterflashing, and on the outside by turning down at least 2″ with a drip edge along the bottom.

Another way to help take the threat of water intrusion off the ledge would be to design a gutter system to drain all of the water coming off the tile roof above.

Design Principle   Control water runoff whenever possible.

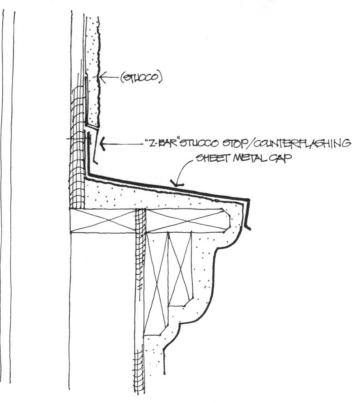

(STUCCO)

"Z-BAR" STUCCO STOP/COUNTERFLASHING
SHEET METAL CAP

Sheet metal cap is possibly open to water entry

Observation   An HVAC unit was properly resting on a curb cap made of sheet metal, but the opening that allowed for condensate and conduit pipes was not handled properly and left the entire curb open below to possible moisture intrusion. The capsheet that is showing within the opening may cover the entire curb, but, even if it does, the edge of the opening should be sealed against moisture.

If any moisture was present beneath the metal, it could start oxidation and/or corrosion on the underside, eventually leading to rusting out of the cap.

Recommendation   Any seams in the metal should be a standing-seam or a flat-lock seam that will allow for expansion and contraction, yet remain water-tight. The hood for the conduit/pipes should be integrated with the remaining sheet metal so that they can move with ease and still not allow moisture intrusion.

The HVAC unit should be permanently affixed to the cap also, so that vibratory movements can be virtually eliminated. This will minimize the chances of the conduit breaking loose at the vertical connections going down through the curb.

Design Principle   Don't leave design decisions to field personnel.

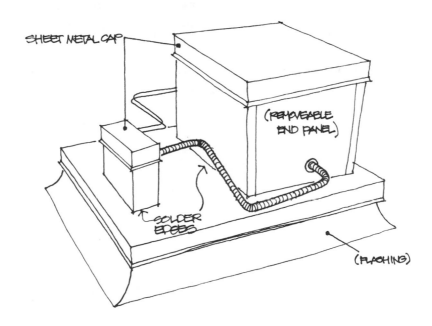

SHEET METAL CAP

(REMOVEABLE END PANEL)

SOLDER EDGES

(FLASHING)

Leaks occurring below conduit penetration

Observation Conduits with flexible connections at the roof level are supposedly flashed with rigid sheet metal, yet do not prevent water entry below. Repair attempts have been made, evidenced by the excessive amount of roofing cement around each pipe. (Note empty roofing cement can and trowel used and discarded—poor roofing practices in all areas!)

Recommendation Install a hooded-type cover over all ganged-pipe connections. This will keep out possible water intrusion and leave an opening large enough to allow movement by the flexible hoses going through the roof below.

Design Principle Do not rely on roofing cement as the sole waterproofing.

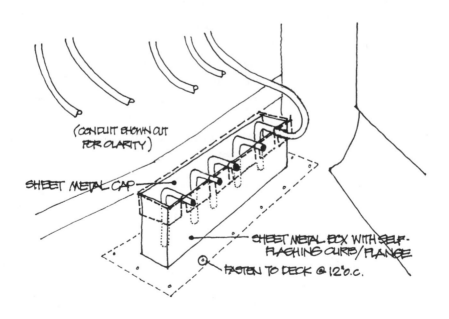

(CONDUIT SHOWN OUT FOR CLARITY)

SHEET METAL CAP

SHEET METAL BOX WITH SELF-FLASHING CURB/FLANGE

FASTEN TO DECK @ 12"o.c.

Exhaust hood is taking on water

Observation The open side of an exhaust hood is facing up the slope of a smooth-surface built-up roof, allowing water to enter in a virtually unrestricted fashion. The only prevention is the small (¾" high) lip along the bottom of the mouth of the opening. No flashing was applied when the roof was installed either. The top ply of roofing was simply cut off at the base of the sheet metal hood and mopped into place.

Recommendation First of all, the hood should be raised to a minimum height of 8" above the uphill side of the roof. The most obvious and effective action taken would be to remove the hood and simply turn it around so that the open side of the hood faces downhill, thereby alleviating any direct water entry possibilities. After the curb is built and the hood turned around, the method of flashing should follow standard NRCA details, whether the system in place is a built-up, single-ply, or modified bitumen variety.

Design Principle Specify all curbs to have a minimum 8" height.

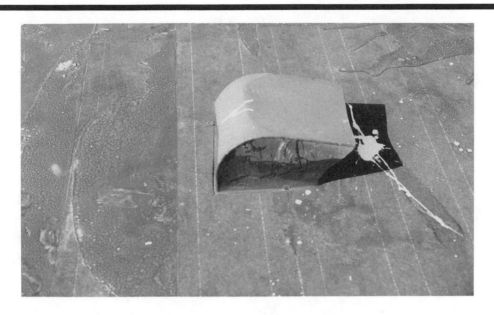

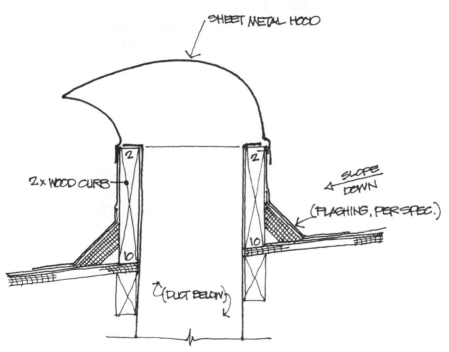

SHEET METAL HOOD

2 x WOOD CURB

2

2

SLOPE DOWN

(FLASHING, PER SPEC.)

10

10

(DUCT BELOW)

Kitchen grease attacks roof membrane

Observation A large exhaust fan, located over a cooking grille in a kitchen window, is dumping residue from burned animal fats and vegetable oils onto the roofing system, causing rapid deterioration of the capsheet. As the roof membrane begins to disintegrate, the cracks in the uppermost surface eventually begin to transfer down through the plies, allowing water entry below.

Recommendation Cooking oils are detrimental to asphalt-based roofing material, as they are with EPDM (ethylene propylene diene monomer) synthetic rubber roofing. In either system, the best solution is to catch the oils and grease before they have a chance to hit the roof membrane. This can be accomplished by specifying a sand box to be incorporated into the fan's base so that a catch basin can be made for the grease falling onto the sand, and changing the box periodically with a fresh supply of sand. Specify regular roof maintenance as part of the warranty requirements, and include monitoring the condition of the grease trap.

Design Principle Be aware of special conditions created on the roof by the equipment that is to be in use and design accordingly.

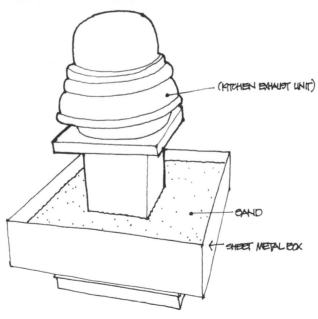

(KITCHEN EXHAUST UNIT)

SAND

SHEET METAL BOX

31

Mechanical equipment is inadequately flashed

Observation
Not having been covered in the project documents, this refrigeration unit and its electrical circuit box have been mounted on the roof surface in a rather unorthodox fashion. Nailing wood bases directly onto the roof surface and covering them with roofing cement will not keep water out of the areas below.

Electrical circuitry exposed to rain can be dangerous because of the threat of short circuits and possible fire. Also, wind can easily get under the sheet metal cover on the main unit and blow it off, causing further damage as it somersaults across the roof by piercing holes with each corner.

Recommendation
A roof curb should have been detailed, having a sheet metal cap and a sheet metal box for the unit so that it could be maintained easily and still be protected from the elements. By having a removeable top on the box, maintenance can be performed without affecting the main waterproofing curb. This could be secured onto the box with a single sheet metal screw with a neoprene washer fastened on each of the four vertical sides.

Design Principle
Don't leave design decisions to field personnel.

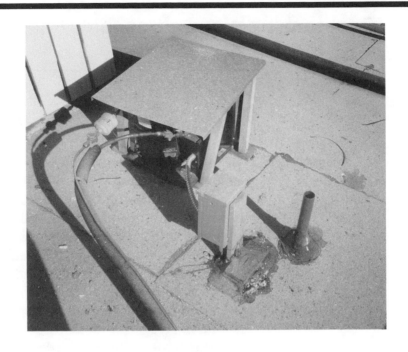

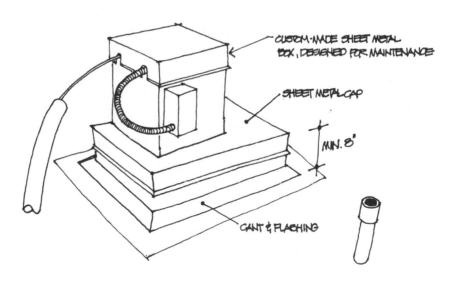

CUSTOM-MADE SHEET METAL BOX, DESIGNED FOR MAINTENANCE

SHEET METAL CAP

MIN. 8"

CANT & FLASHING

Door leaking along threshold

Observation   It was discovered that water was coming in at the termination of a base flashing condition that ended rather abruptly at a door jamb. Even the surface-mounted counterflashing just died out at the end, with no proper termination method other than field-applied caulking. This results in a high-maintenance condition that will only worsen with time. The factory door threshold was not used, and in its place was a field-fabricated sheet metal threshold that did not fit in at all well with the door jamb on each of its ends.

Recommendation   Specify that the roofing and its flashing be installed prior to the installation of both the door and the counterflashing. This way the wall flashing can turn back inside and have the threshold installed over it, and a bead of caulk can keep the first attack of water away from the inside of the door jamb. The door threshold itself should have been installed higher to alleviate the chance of standing water blowing up and over such a low threshold, as is now existing.

Design Principle   Design flashing details at the juncture of dissimilar materials.

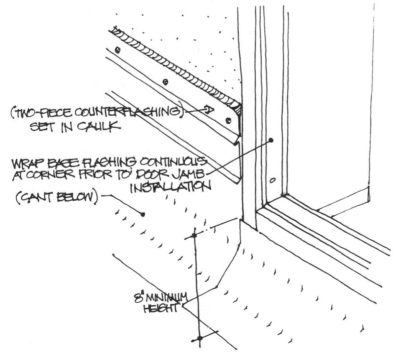

(TWO-PIECE COUNTERFLASHING)
SET IN CAULK

WRAP BASE FLASHING CONTINUOUS
AT CORNER PRIOR TO DOOR JAMB
INSTALLATION

(CANT BELOW)

8" MINIMUM
HEIGHT

End wall was not flashed having open gutter above

Observation	A detail showing the termination of shingles was not included in the project's architectural plans. Consequently, the method of installation was left to the discretion of the shingle applicator. As a result, the end of the wall was left open to probable water entry.
	To exacerbate the situation, there is a gutter with an open end situated directly above this condition that will only add water to an existing problem.
Recommendation	Initially, roofing felt should have been installed continuously around the end of the wall. The shingles would then terminate as they do now. Then a one-piece flashing of sheet metal would be installed at the end of the wall, lapping each wall of the shingles a minimum of 4" and set in a ¼" bed of roofing cement.
	The gutter above should not have been left open. It should have extended out and had a downspout and gutter take the water to a splash block below.
	Don't ever let the water draining from a roof above fall directly onto the roofing surface, no matter what type of material. A splash block will afford all the necessary protection for the life of the roof.
Design Principle	Control water runoff when possible.

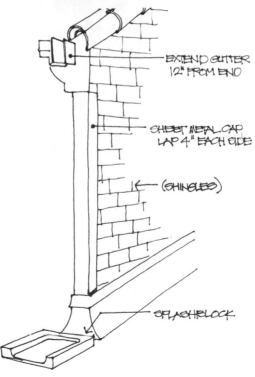

EXTEND GUTTER
12" FROM END

SHEET METAL CAP
LAP 4" EACH SIDE

(SHINGLES)

SPLASHBLOCK

Television antenna punctures roof

Observation A television antenna had been attached to a vent pipe on a commercial store and had been blown over in a windstorm. The result was a small, but deep, hole where the metal rib penetrated the roofing system on impact, thereby causing an immediate leak during the following rain.

Recommendation The antenna should be attached to a formidable vertical surface, preferably the parapet wall, as shown in the background of the picture. Even attaching the antenna to its own base would be difficult because of the size the base would have to be on the roof. The antenna is extremely top-heavy and is susceptible to overturning.

The antenna should be mounted onto a base that has itself been mounted securely to the wall. In this case, a piece of 3/4" plywood fastened to the masonry wall with expanding bolts should suffice, followed by flashing with the same material the wall is flashed with. Then when the antenna is mounted to the base, set any fasteners for clamps in a bed of modified mastic for a proper sealing technique.

Design Principle Specify and detail rooftop accessory items to be attached and flashed permanently along outside walls.

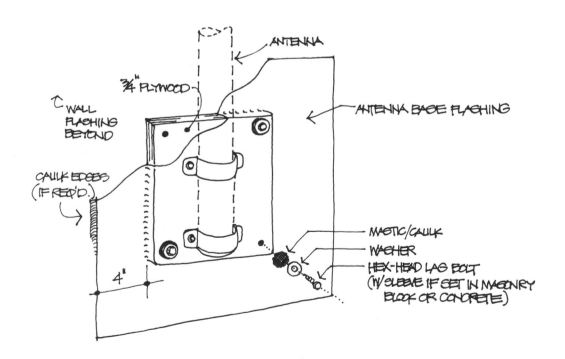

ANTENNA

¾" PLYWOOD

WALL
FLASHING
BEYOND

ANTENNA BASE FLASHING

CAULK EDGES
(IF REQ'D.)

4"

MASTIC/CAULK

WASHER

HEX-HEAD LAG BOLT
(W/SLEEVE IF SET IN MASONRY
BLOCK OR CONCRETE)

Leaking at ladder stanchions

Observation Leaks were discovered below where the roof access ladder was located. The steel ladder had been attached to the roof and simply mopped around when the roofing system was installed. Roofing mastic was the only material depended on to prevent water entry at the points where the ladder penetrated the roof membrane. But the vibrations in the ladder's steel frame caused the mastic to break loose at the roof level, consequently allowing water entry.

Recommendation The ladder should have been mounted on the inside vertical surface of the parapet wall. This way, no matter how it is mounted, the penetration made for securing the ladder stanchions are on something other than the roof surface, and it is simply not as easy for water to enter the areas below.

Ideally, the wall flashing should be applied first, and the ladder base mounted in a bed of modified mastic, with screw-type fasteners securing the base to the wall. The mastic, modified with polymers, allows a little more movement than regular mastic and will better handle the movement from the vibrations sent through the ladder every time it is used for roof access.

Design Principle Penetrate roof area in vertical planes when possible.

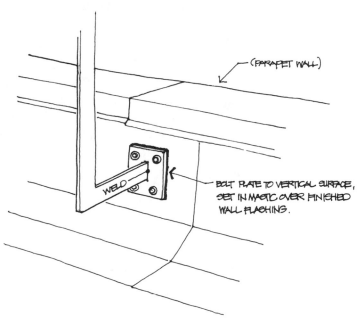

(PARAPET WALL)

WELD

BOLT PLATE TO VERTICAL SURFACE,
SET IN MASTIC OVER FINISHED
WALL FLASHING.

Leaking at capsheet flashing

Observation Leaks were noted at the corner/edge of a gravel-surfaced roof where it intersected with a cedar shake roof. A small parapet wall bordered the built-up roof area and was flashed with a regular 72-lb. granular surface capsheet. Water had entered the walls at a number of locations, mostly centered around where the capsheet was installed in non-planar areas. It appeared that the capsheet flashing did not bend very well and simply fractured along the axes of the folds and bends.

Recommendation If the design demands that the flashing cover any angles and bends that are out of the normal realm of edge configurations, it is best to specify a flashing that has both the reinforcement and the pliability built in, so that any shape or movement can be adequately handled by the flashing material. In this case, a spunbonded polyester reinforcement would give adequate support to a modified bitumen sheet and would have worked better than a normal, unreinforced capsheet.

Design Principle Don't leave design decisions to field personnel.

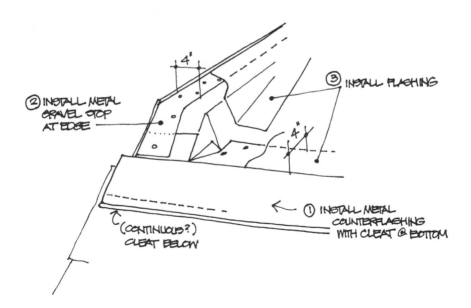

② INSTALL METAL GRAVEL STOP AT EDGE

4"

③ INSTALL FLASHING

4"

(CONTINUOUS?) CLEAT BELOW

① INSTALL METAL COUNTERFLASHING WITH CLEAT @ BOTTOM

37

Leaking at parapet wall

Observation Water is entering a building below due to open edges of the wall flashing intersecting with the gravel stop flashing. Their junction is susceptible to building movement, and it appears that the roofing materials alone will not accommodate the demands placed on the flashing to keep the water out. There is no sheet metal flashing, except for the gravel stop.

Recommendation Metal coping should have been installed along the top of the small parapet wall. The flashing below then should have been terminated with either a sheet metal cap or a mechanical bar termination at the corner. Then the gravel stop flashing could be tied in with the wall flashing and make a continuous waterstop along the edge. For ease of application, the cant strip along the parapet wall could be angle-cut a few inches away from the end to facilitate the flashing's transition.

Design Principle Don't leave design decisions to field personnel.

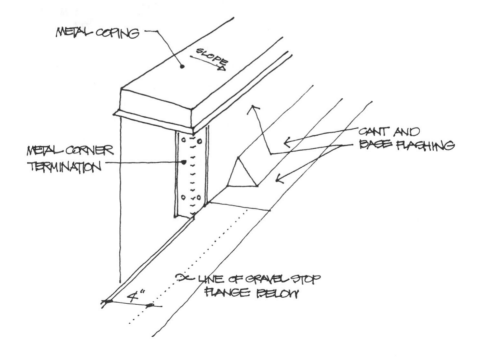

METAL COPING

SLOPE

METAL CORNER
TERMINATION

CANT AND
BASE FLASHING

LINE OF GRAVEL STOP
FLANGE BELOW

4"

Leaking at wall intersections

Observation   Leaks had been reported, and repairs had been attempted (to no avail), at an area of the roof where a small parapet wall intersected a perimeter parapet wall. The small wall was covered in capsheet roofing material and was simply terminated and sealed with roofing cement at the end where it dead-ended into the sheet metal on the higher wall.

Recommendation   A treated wood nailer should have been called for along the top of the small wall, along with a sheet metal coping to cap it. Then the metal coping could have been turned up underneath the metal on the higher wall, resulting in a much more watertight situation, and one that could easier take the inevitable movement incurred at this condition.

Design Principle   Don't leave design decisions to field personnel.

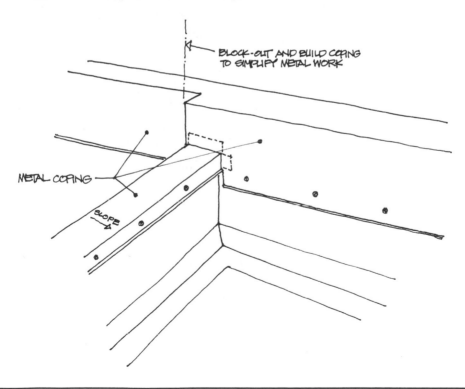

BLOCK-OUT AND BUILD COPING
TO SIMPLIFY METAL WORK

METAL COPING

SLOPE

Antenna wire is anchored through coping

Observation   A television antenna wire had been secured to a spiral metal loop that had been fastened through the coping into the wood nailer below for stability. Since the coping was designed and installed as flat, water tended to stand all along the coping when it rained, and consistently leaked into the area below the wall.

Recommendation   First of all, the penetration should not have been made in the horizontal surface of the coping. But this detail was not called out in the project documents, leaving it's method of flashing up to the installer. It would have been just as easy to have gone into the back side of the coping (on the vertical surface) and still anchored into the nailer. Then the chance of water entry could have been reduced considerably. Flashing around the penetration is then easily done on an area that water is not standing in waiting to enter below.

Adding a positive slope to the metal coping is one of the most basic ways to minimize water entry problems, simply due to the fact that water is moving off the coping the minute it hits the top of the metal.

Design Principle   Specify and detail rooftop accessory items to be attached and flashed permanently along outside walls.

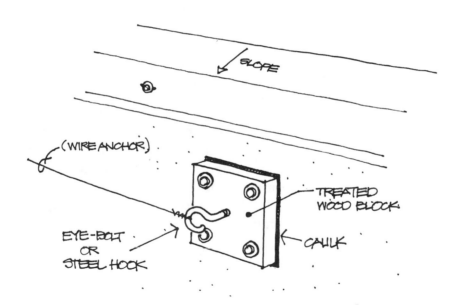

SLOPE

(WIRE ANCHOR)

TREATED
WOOD BLOCK

EYE-BOLT
OR
STEEL HOOK

CAULK

Leaks at wall change

Observation   A small parapet, flashed with capsheet roofing material and capped with clay tile, butted into a higher masonry block wall in the same plane. The resulting intersection had wood, masonry, clay tile, mastic, and sheet metal all trying to act in concert with one another and keep water out. This, however, was a failure and water easily entered the building directly below this intersection. There was no provision made for counterflashing or the lapping of materials, relying all the while on roofing cement to secure the material's edges and prevent moisture intrusion.

Recommendation   Through-wall metal counterflashing should have been installed in a two-piece fashion above both the clay tile and the base flashing for the adjoining roof. A short transition piece of sheet metal could have then been incorporated into the flashing to terminate the parapet wall covering.

Design Principle   Design flashing details at the juncture of dissimilar materials.

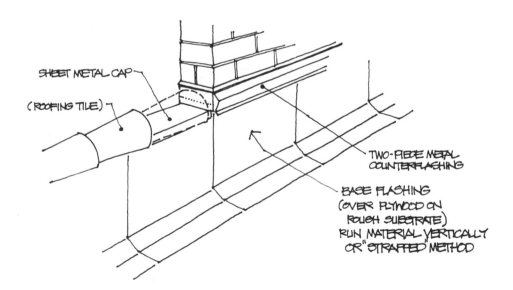

SHEET METAL CAP

(ROOFING TILE)

TWO-PIECE METAL
COUNTERFLASHING

BASE FLASHING
(OVER PLYWOOD ON
ROUGH SUBSTRATE)
RUN MATERIAL VERTICALLY
OR "STRAPPED" METHOD

Deterioration of structural wall support

Observation   A rather large C-section was required to lend supplementary support to a rather short parapet wall. However, over the years, the locations of the through-wall bolts penetrating the wall also allowed water entry, rusting the bolts themselves and transferring same to the structural member. Repairs were attempted all along the wall in futile efforts to stop the moisture intrusion, but to no avail.

Recommendation   Being that the steel section was added as an afterthought, the roofing membrane did not have the proper conditions in turning up the wall. A 90° angle was made by the wall flashing, something that built-up materials are not made to do successfully, and the area's repair was impossible due to the permanent installation of the support.

Basically, a box could have been made out of the steel section and cants added to where the roofing material could have gone from the outer edge (at a gravel stop) to the field of the roof, making successful transitions via cant strips. With the outer nailer sloped toward the inside, water now is directed in a positive fashion to the field of the roof and on to positive drainage at the roof drains.

Design Principle   Provide details at the juncture of dissimilar materials.

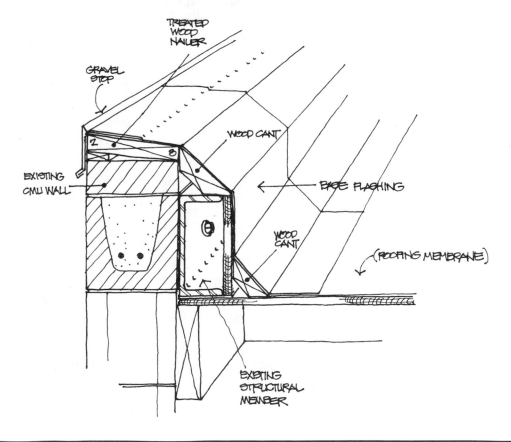

TREATED
WOOD
NAILER

GRAVEL
STOP

WOOD CANT

EXISTING
CMU WALL

BASE FLASHING

WOOD
CANT

(ROOFING MEMBRANE)

EXISTING
STRUCTURAL
MEMBER

42

Flashing was improperly installed on parapet wall

Observation   A regular granular-surface capsheet was found to be covering, in a somewhat unorthodox fashion, the end of a parapet wall. Many cracks were discovered to be contributing to leaks reported below, as were the many uncovered nail holes made by the fasteners in the cap-sheet. Also, the horizontal method of installation pictured in the problem photograph tends to lead to sagging material, due to the fact that it cannot hold itself up.

Recommendation   The roofing material needs to be terminated just above the field of the roof, secured, and separated from the flashing material used on the walls. The wall flashing needs to be terminated at the outside edge, and this termination method needs to be protected, thereby requiring sheet metal coping to go over the end of the wall flashing at the top of the wall.

Any wall over 24" in height should have specifications to direct the installer to "strap" the walls vertically, and the bottom piece of material nailed 6" o.c. vertically at the lap, so that the next overlapping piece can properly cover the fasteners. This ensures that the flashing will remain stationary and perform as required.

Design Principle   Don't leave design decisions to field personnel.

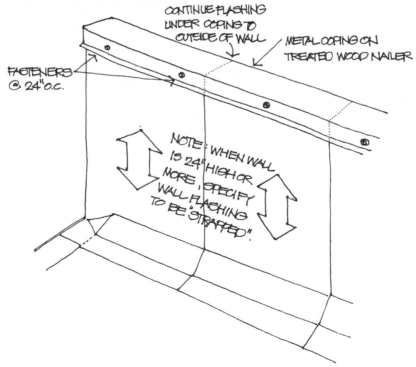

CONTINUE FLASHING
UNDER COPING TO
OUTSIDE OF WALL

METAL COPING ON
TREATED WOOD NAILER

FASTENERS
@ 24" o.c.

NOTE: WHEN WALL
IS 24" HIGH OR
MORE, SPECIFY
WALL FLASHING
TO BE "STRAPPED"

43

Ladder was inadequately secured at roof edge

Observation On inspecting a roof, it was noted that the roof access ladder was loose and not anchored into the parapet wall except for a couple of lag bolts placed haphazardly into a two-by-four that had simply been nailed into the stucco finish and the metal coping above it. This made climbing down especially hard, since the whole platform used to start the descent was not secure, causing a possibly dangerous situation.

Recommendation Mount the ladder on the inside of the wall, especially along the studs if it is a wood frame construction. The ends of the ladder should be welded onto a plate and that in turn should be affixed to the wall after the wall flashing has been applied. This way the penetrations created by the anchor bolts can be properly secured into something that will not allow water intrusion at their points of entry.

Design Principle Don't penetrate the roof unnecessarily.

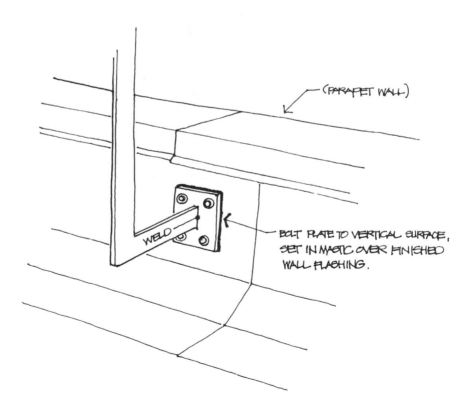

(PARAPET WALL)

WELD

BOLT PLATE TO VERTICAL SURFACE,
SET IN MASTIC OVER FINISHED
WALL FLASHING.

Leaks at corner of concrete parapet wall

Observation   Repairs had been attempted at the junction of two precast concrete walls where the wall flashing had simply been turned out over the top of the wall and nailed into the concrete. Even though a thick caulking joint on the outside of the wall had split and was allowing some water entry, the majority of the leaks were attributed to water entering at the top of the wall.

Recommendation   In order to terminate the wall flashing, a treated wood nailer should have been installed along the top of the wall at the entire perimeter of the roof, sloped toward the interior. Then the flashing should have been taken to the outside edge of the nailer and mechanically fastened. Once in place, the metal coping should be installed and fastened off through the inside vertical face. This way, when future repair or re-roofing work is done, the coping can be safely removed and put back into place, extending the useful life of both the roof and the coping.

Design Principle   Always use a wood nailer along tops of walls for flashing termination.

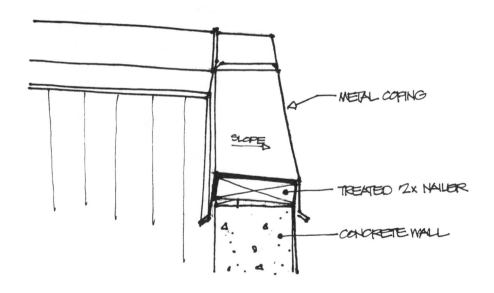

METAL COPING

SLOPE

TREATED 2x NAILER

CONCRETE WALL

Small parapet wall is open to water entry

Observation A short parapet wall ended at a roof level change, and numerous leaks were reported below. The metal gravel stop nailed into the top of the wall was not flashed, same as the cap flashing turning the corner of the wall and stopping with no proper termination. Even repair attempts had not been sufficient to stop the water from entering the building.

Recommendation All edges of planes of the roof and wall should have been terminated properly. This should have been done with a metal coping on top of the parapet wall, a metal edge at the end of the wall, and a metal gravel stop on the end of the roof level just below, terminating that roof. A detail was not shown in the original project documents, so the flashing decision was left up to the contractor installing the roof. You can plainly see the fallacy in allowing that to happen.

Design Principle Don't leave design decisions to field personnel.

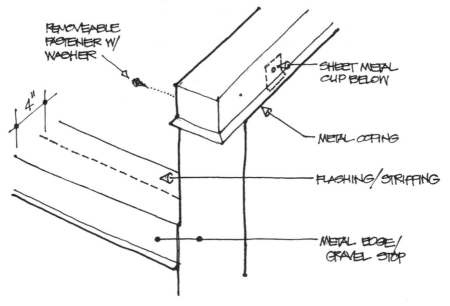

REMOVEABLE FASTENER W/ WASHER

SHEET METAL CLIP BELOW

4"

METAL COPING

FLASHING/STRIPPING

METAL EDGE/ GRAVEL STOP

46

Roofing material is bridging at HVAC curb

Observation   PVC roofing material has become taut along the edge of an HVAC unit. Natural shrinkage of material is now exaggerated at the mechanical curb due to lack of proper termination at changes of roofing planes.

Recommendation   Roofing material in field should be terminated at the edge of the plane that the roof lies in (along the bottom of the HVAC curb), and the flashing material used on the HVAC curb should cover the termination points of the lowest plane's material. The top of the curb should be covered in sheet metal—one piece if the curb size allows such and the use of a standing-seam joint if one is necessary.

Design Principle   Terminate and flash each change of plane of a roof.

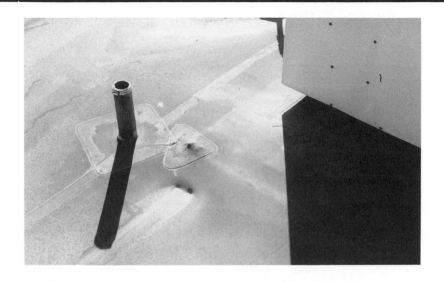

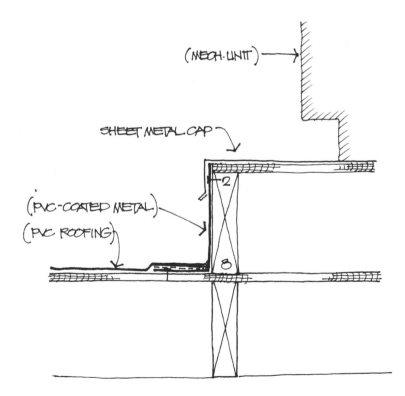

(MECH. UNIT) ⟶

SHEET METAL CAP

(PVC-COATED METAL)

(PVC ROOFING)

Mechanical curb is too low

Observation   The mechanical curb is too close to the roof surface and will easily allow water entry if a blowing rainstorm occurs. Under the guise of saving money during the original installation, the contractor who installed the curb only used a two-by-four above the plywood deck surface. Once the built-up roofing was installed, it dropped the effective height of the top of the curb to less than 5" above the roof surface.

Recommendation   Either during the design phase of the building or whenever the building is re-roofed, the NRCA recommends at least an 8" curb height above the finished roof surface, especially in areas where it snows and drifting can occur. Using at least a two-by-eight should suffice, and a two-by-ten would work even better. The cost difference between the minimum and the preferred is minute when compared to the trouble that is avoided over the life of the roof.

Design Principle   Design all curb heights a minimum of 8" above the roof.

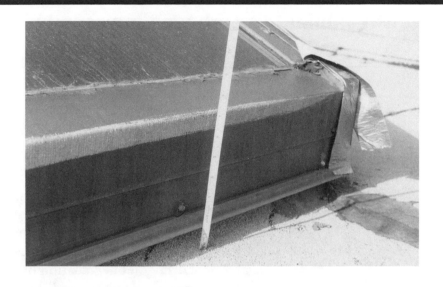

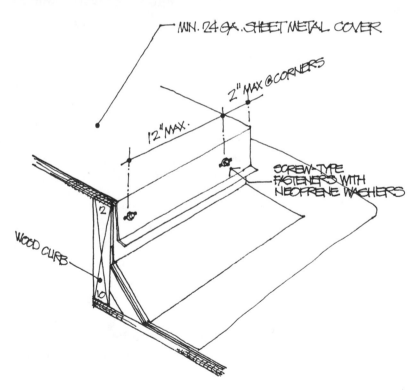

MIN. 24 GA. SHEET METAL COVER

2" MAX @ CORNERS

12" MAX.

SCREW-TYPE
FASTENERS WITH
NEOPRENE WASHERS

WOOD CURB

Pre-fabricated curb was improperly installed

Observation   Mechanical equipment curb is simply sitting on a two-by-four, with roofing mastic applied in hopes of preventing possible water entry. Common nails were used to fasten the unit through the wood nailer directly into the plywood roof deck. Now leaks have occurred at the points of fastening. Ultraviolet degradation has caused splits in the roofing mastic, and it is no longer able to properly seal the mechanical unit's flange.

Recommendation   The unit, as installed, had hardly any chance of keeping water out from its installation. Had a properly designed curb detail been shown in the architect's drawings, the roofing contractor would have had a guideline for flashing in the unit adequately. As it was, the decision on how to flash the curb was left to the discretion of the laborer.

What should have been done was to have set the primed flange in a ¼" bed of roofing mastic on top of the roofing plies, fastened it securely to the deck with screws, and flashed it in. Ideally, a polyester-reinforced modified bitumen, either APP (Atactic Polypropylene) or SBS(Styrene-Butadiene-Styrene), would be best to use in that conditon to allow for any movement brought about by the on-and-off cyclic vibration of the mechanical unit in operation.

Design Principle   Provide individual details for each different curb.

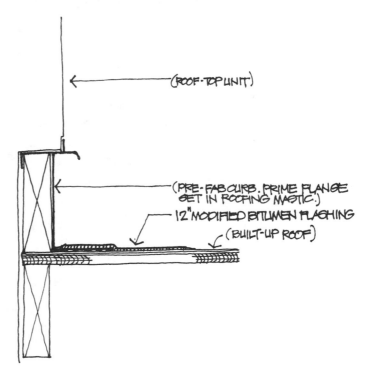

(ROOF-TOP UNIT)

(PRE-FAB CURB. PRIME FLANGE
SET IN ROOFING MASTIC.)

12" MODIFIED BITUMEN FLASHING

(BUILT-UP ROOF)

49

Base flashing has fractured along curb

Observation   The base flashing along the curb of the roof hatch has split from either not being full adhered, thereby bridging from the horizontal to the vertical planes and then being stepped on, or as a result of tensile forces on a dynamic roof surface simply pulling the flashing material apart. This can also happen sometimes when a cant is not installed and the bituminous roofing material is required to make a 90° turn. Most any other roofing systems can do this without a cant.

Recommendation   Areas most likely to cause problems on any roof are at the points where the roof goes from horizontal to vertical—the edges, curbs, and penetrations. This is where the specifier can protect the roof from problems by making sure that the material is designed to withstand the forces brought on it in the performance of a roofing system.

A spunbonded polyester and/or fiberglass reinforcement is good to have in the areas most needed to give the flashing material some added ability to withstand the demands from the surrounding forces and elements.

Design Principle   Most leaks occur at edges and penetrations.

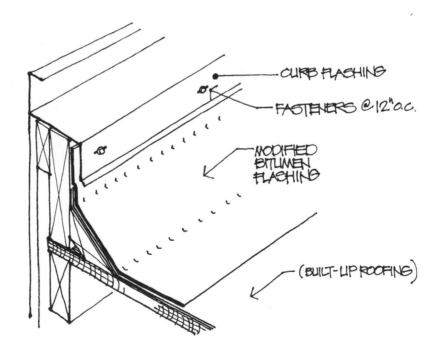

CURB FLASHING

FASTENERS @ 12" o.c.

MODIFIED BITUMEN FLASHING

(BUILT-UP ROOFING)

Water is ponding behind mechanical curb

Observation   The roof is sloping toward the back side of a mechanical curb, which is itself dangerously low (4") even without the ponding. And being a rather long curb, water has no diversion to get around the curb, so water will accumulate along the base of the curb flashing. If strong winds were to accompany a rainstorm, this condition could easily send water up and over the curb and into the interior.

Recommendation   All curbs should have "crickets" (water diverters), designed into the upslope side to avoid situations such as this. Crickets can be installed with either plywood below built directly onto the deck, or on top of the roofing membrane in the form of tapered insulation, and simply flashed over. The top of the curb should then be at least 4" higher than the high point of the cricket, to alleviate the possibilities of water entry.

Design Principle   Positive slope prevents ponding conditions.

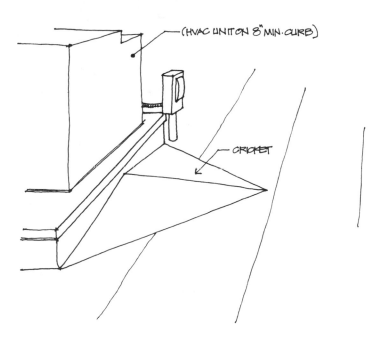

(HVAC UNIT ON 8" MIN. CURB)

CRICKET

51

Pre-fabricated curb was improperly installed

Observation A pre-fabricated curb was specified, but not detailed as to how it was to be installed, and a curb was built in the field, only to have the factory unit simply perch on top of it and be expected to work. Leaks occurred when the exposed wood fiber insulation, installed at the factory, began to take on water around the curb and pass it on to the interior. No provision was made in the contract documents as to how this was to be protected.

Recommendation It would appear that common sense would have told someone on the job site, as they were installing this curb, that something was amiss. But intangible factors, such as schedules, availability of workers, and delivery of materials can create nightmares on their own. But you, as an architect and specifier, cannot assume anything out of your control to happen for the good, so you must extend your control as easily and efficiently as possible.

It is usually best to remove or cover over the factory-installed insulation. It has little or no insulating value, so putting plywood in its place gives the roofing a much better surface on which to apply his flashing material.

Design Principle Provide individual details for each different curb.

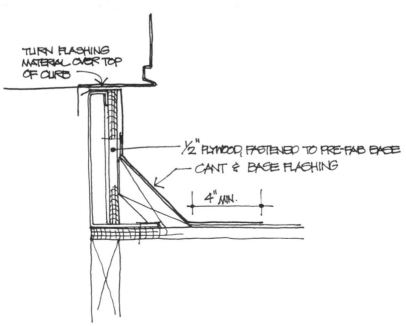

TURN FLASHING
MATERIAL OVER TOP
OF CURB

½" PLYWOOD, FASTENED TO PRE-FAB BASE

CANT & BASE FLASHING

4" MIN.

Mechanical ducts were not properly flashed

Observation Two mechanical ducts penetrating a roof were found to be letting in water at some point, and repairs were attempted. Even though these curbs are probably self-flashing, if they leak then there is something wrong with their installation. One obvious anomaly is the fact that, no matter how they are flashed, they are too close together.

Recommendation First and foremost, the curbs should be raised to at least an 8" minimum height at the upslope side of the curb. Second, they should be at least 18" apart in order to flash them properly. The fasteners used to hold the sheet metal curb cap in place should only be installed on the vertical surfaces so as to prevent water entry. If the unit's curbs are self-flashing, it would still be wise to have them up out of the plane of the finished roof surface.

Design Principle Keep all penetrations up out of the roof plane.

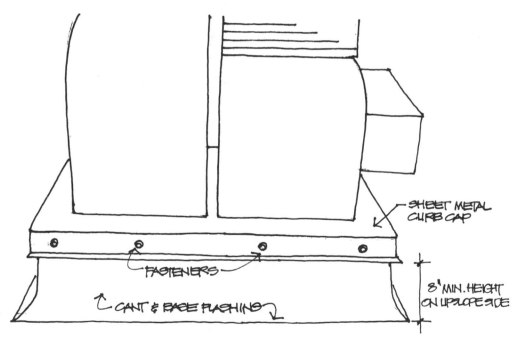

SHEET METAL
CURB CAP

FASTENERS

CANT & BASE FLASHING

8" MIN. HEIGHT
ON UPSLOPE SIDE

Air-conditioning units have vibrated off their isolation pads

Observation Mechanical air-handling units have moved so much with their constant on-and-off cycling that they managed to topple from the spring-type pads designed to allow for this very movement. The trouble is that these pads themselves are not fastened at all, and consequently move when the units move. This is compounded by the fact that the flexible hoses carrying air and freon back and forth to these units are themselves not flashed into the roof properly. So, when the units and their hoses move around, an opening is created at the penetration point of the roof.

Recommendation Two items are of equal importance here: how the units are secured and how the hoses enter the building at the roof. The units should each be placed on a curb with a minimum height of 8". Then a metal cap should cover the curb and have the unit fastened into the metal cap.

Secondly, the hoses coming up from inside should be gathered into one entry location and covered with a rain hood. This way the hoses are free to move and are watertight at the same time.

Design Principle Don't expect a mechanical contractor to flash a roof penetration. Do it with a detail.

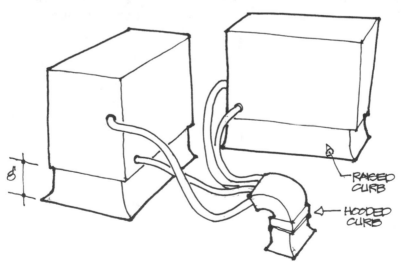

RAISED CURB

HOODED CURB

54

Vent pipe is too close to wall

Observation   A vent pipe has been installed too close to a higher wall. Being hard to flash pipe properly, it is equally hard to flash the wall along the counterflashing. Leaking at this location is now a strong possibility.

Either the architect did not properly coordinate plumbing plans with architectural plans, the mechanical engineer missed the location and coordination of a proximate wall, or a quality control (field) inspector was not present during installation.

Recommendation   Scrape the existing gravel back 12" from each side of the vent pipe and install a new lead boot, stripping-in the flanges of the lead boot to the roofing and turning the flange nearest the wall up under the counterflashing and fastening it.

In a new building design, keep all roof penetrations a minimum of 18" away from any other penetrations or changes in roofing planes. If proximate penetrations are electrical conduits and must be close together, they can be flashed with a hooded metal cover.

Design Principle   Provide enough space between penetrations to allow the contractor ample room to flash properly.

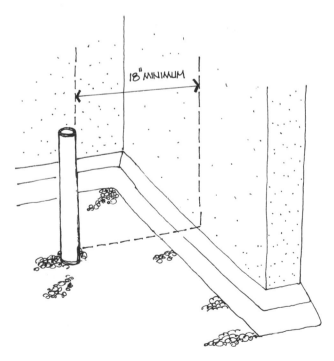

18" MINIMUM

Vent pipe was not flashed adequately

Observation Mastic applied as sole source of waterproofing has dried out, and the resulting crack has left the interior of the building open to possible water intrusion. This could have been avoided by specifying and/or installing the proper flashing.

Recommendation Either during the design phase or during a post-installation condition, a 4-lb. lead boot with a lead cap is best suited to prevent water entry. The boot should be set in a bed of roofing cement, fastened through the flange into the roof deck, stripped-in with overlapping plies of roofing felt, and covered with a sheet of modified bitumen.

Design Principle Design a roof with long-term, low maintenance components in mind.

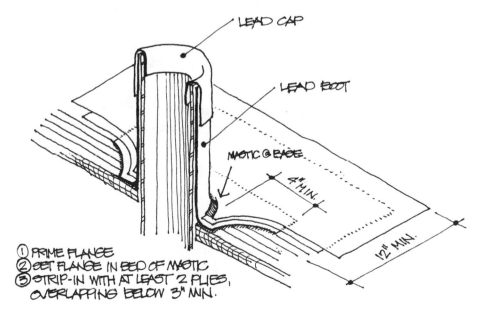

LEAD CAP

LEAD BOOT

MASTIC @ BASE

4" MIN.

12" MIN.

① PRIME FLANGE
② SET FLANGE IN BED OF MASTIC
③ STRIP-IN WITH AT LEAST 2 PLIES,
OVERLAPPING BELOW 3" MIN.

56

Vent pipe is leaking at shingles

Observation   A cast iron vent pipe protruding through shingles has mastic applied around its base as the sole source protection against water entry. Because it is not blocked off below, the pipe has a tendency to move about rather freely within the opening around the shingles. Also, the pipe has been cut off too close to the finished roof level. It should be at least 8" above the uphill side.

Recommendation   Being that this is cast iron, an extension should be spot-welded onto the existing pipe to bring it up to proper height. Then a 4-lb. lead boot and lead cap should be installed as flashing over the pipe and lapping under the shingles. The flange of the boot should be set in a bed of mastic and nailed on the uncovered flanges with fasteners at 6" o.c.

Design Principle   Treat penetrations of all sizes with equal attention to waterproofing capabilities.

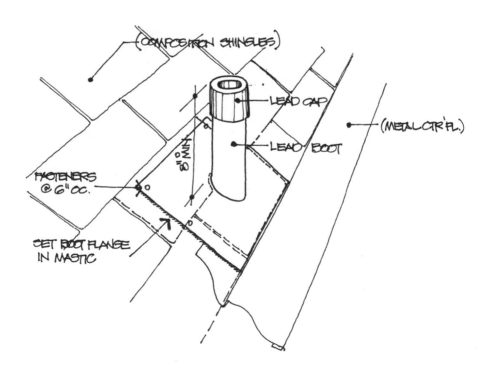

(COMPOSITION SHINGLES)

LEAD CAP

(METAL CTR'FL.)

LEAD BOOT

8" MIN.

FASTENERS
@ 6" O.C.

SET BOOT FLANGE
IN MASTIC

Vent pipes are too close to edge

Observation Vent pipes lead up from back-to-back bathrooms below and now contribute to leaks in each bathroom wall due to a failed flashing attempt. The proximity to the roof's level change has left each pipe with little or no room for proper flashing. The movement between the adjacent roof levels has also caused the mastic around the vents to crack, thereby making water entry a constant possibility. In addition, this condition makes proper flashing of the level change impossible, due to the interruption of the gravel stop above and the base flashing of the roof area below.

Recommendation The vent pipes should be kept back from the edge of the roof, or any other penetration for that matter, at least 18". Any less is still possible to flash, but the chances of doing so successfully are reduced. And not only should the pipes be kept away from each other, but proper spacing from the roof edge allows that area to have a decent chance of preventing moisture intrusion.

Design Principle Provide enough space between penetrations to allow the contractor ample room to flash properly.

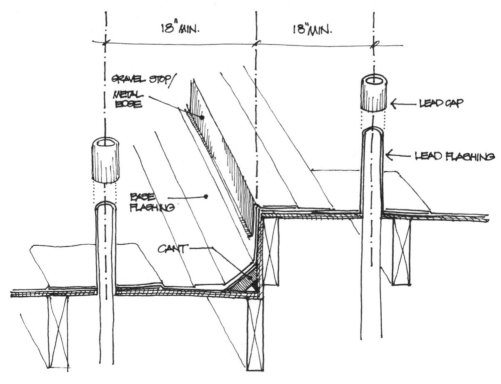

Single-ply membrane is bridging at higher roof

Observation Level change at roof, approximately 18" high, has PVC roofing material stretching from lower level up to higher level without proper termination, causing material to overextend itself. The roofing material has not been properly installed by being separated at the level change, resulting in tension from one plane to the next.

Recommendation Both top and bottom planes of roofing should be fastened along the edge with mechanical termination and flashed with separate material. Also, another piece of similar material should be used between the upper and lower termination points. This way the two roofing planes are separated and can act independently with regard to their individual movement and requirements.

Design Principle Isolate each roof area as a complete section with flashing.

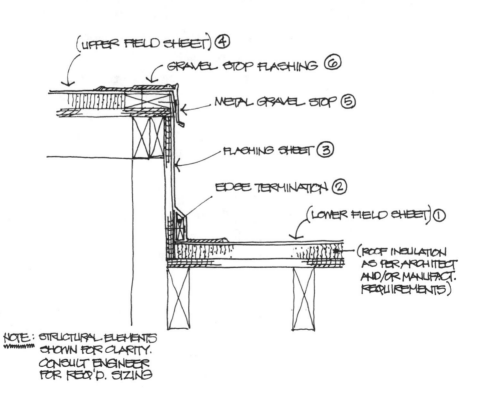

(UPPER FIELD SHEET) ④

GRAVEL STOP FLASHING ⑥

METAL GRAVEL STOP ⑤

FLASHING SHEET ③

EDGE TERMINATION ②

(LOWER FIELD SHEET) ①

(ROOF INSULATION AS PER ARCHITECT AND/OR MANUFACT. REQUIREMENTS)

NOTE: STRUCTURAL ELEMENTS SHOWN FOR CLARITY. CONSULT ENGINEER FOR REQ'D. SIZING

Flashing is leaking at level change

Observation	Parapet walls stepped down along the outside edge of a building on a hillside plot. This resulted in a myriad of various materials and changes of planes. Differential movement occurred in the building's structure, transferring up into the roofing envelope. Consequently, because the roofing could not accept the change in position of its substrate, it failed, as did numerous repair attempts that followed.
Recommendation	In essence, the walls, as the apartment buildings themselves, should have been flashed from the lowest area up to the highest area, in that order. The lower roof's wall flashing should turn up to, and be lapped over by, the upper roof's field material. Then the metal gravel stop can be installed at the edge and flashed in properly, and so on.

Where the flashing material has to be terminated at the vertical edge on the exterior of the building, a metal termination bar, set in mastic, is one good way of preventing unwanted moisture intrusion. This can continue the lap process along the outer edge by being continued over the turned-up metal of the coping below and under the edge of the coping directly above.

Design Principle	Provide details at the juncture of dissimilar materials.

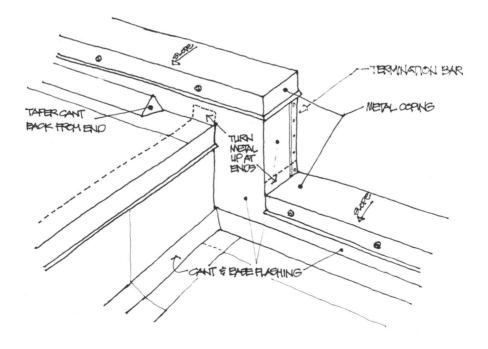

TERMINATION BAR

METAL COPING

TAPER CANT
BACK FROM END

TURN
METAL
UP AT
ENDS

CANT & BASE FLASHING

Leaking at wall termination

Observation   Massive leaks were occurring at the outer edge of a building below an intersection of a low wall, a high wall, and a roof. The architect had not detailed that particular junction of materials and its fate was in the hands of the laborers installing the roofing, the stucco, and the sheet metal. Unless these trades are directed to do certain things to ensure all of their materials work in concert with one another, chances are that the workers of the various trades will not be on the roof at the same time.

Recommendation   As a designer, specify that the roofing gets put on first, that the sheet metal is installed, but removable, and the stucco (a permanent installation) is put on when other trades have all of their materials in place.

In this situation, for instance, the counterflashing should have been a two-piece unit so that the roofing contractor could have at least dried in the roof field and come back to finish the flashing, thereby utilizing the removable metal counterflashing. The metal coping, as now existing, is permanent because of the way the stucco was installed over it. However, by having a clip along the outer edge and screw-type fasteners on the inside edge, the coping theoretically could have been removed had the need arisen.

Design Principle   Don't leave design decisions to field personnel.

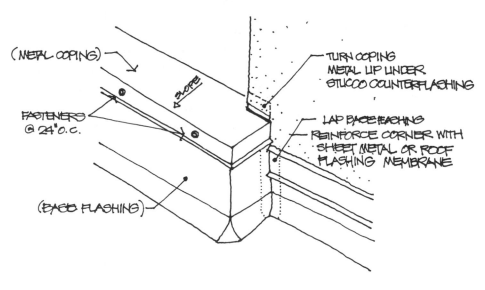

(METAL COPING)

FASTENERS
@ 24" O.C.

SLOPE

(BASE FLASHING)

TURN COPING
METAL LIP UNDER
STUCCO COUNTERFLASHING

LAP BASE FLASHING
REINFORCE CORNER WITH
SHEET METAL OR ROOF
FLASHING MEMBRANE

Roof drain is too close to wall

Observation Both a primary roof drain and an overflow pipe were discovered to have been installed practically flush with an adjacent parapet wall. Cracks were noted in the wall flashing that abutted the clamping ring on the roof drain. Ponding was also observed in the areas proximate to the drain area, evidencing the fact that not all of the water from the roof is reaching the drain area.

Recommendation The roof drains should both be placed in a sump to ensure positive drainage in the area immediately adjacent to the drains, and both the primary and secondary drains should have cast-iron assemblies that include cast-iron strainer baskets. Plastic baskets deteriorate with time and possibly allow debris to enter the drainage system. The overflow drain, whether it is another roof drain or a through-wall scupper, is always to be 2" above the level of the primary drain. The secondary drain pipe leader, if there is one, is to lead into a pipe that is independent of the piping system the primary drain uses.

Design Principle Provide minimum 30" by 30" sump pans for all roof drains.

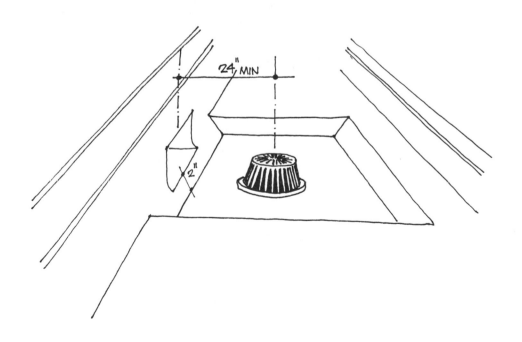

Overflow scupper misses mark

Observation Water run-off from overflow scupper drains partly into the downspout and partly onto the ground. The scupper was designed and/or installed too close to the primary scupper opening through the wall.

Recommendations Specify that the overflow scupper is at least 12" clear, edge-to-edge, of the nearest side of the primary scupper opening. Also, the bottom level of the secondary scupper should be 2" higher than the bottom level of the primary scupper. If the secondary scupper drains into a downspout, it should be linked to a separate drainage system than the primary downspout.

Design Principle Do not leave design decisions to field personnel.

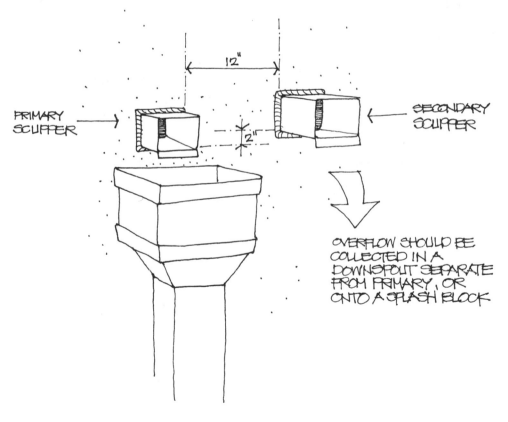

PRIMARY SCUPPER

SECONDARY SCUPPER

12"

2"

OVERFLOW SHOULD BE COLLECTED IN A DOWNSPOUT SEPARATE FROM PRIMARY, OR ONTO A SPLASH BLOCK

63

Roof drainage conflicts with pedestrians

Observation Water from an overflow scupper appears to be headed for the stairs directly below. Pedestrians using the stairs below this scupper will get an extra dose of rain water when a sudden storm arises. This situation requires the use of the secondary scupper.

Recommendation Either move the stairs out farther from the building, allowing the overflow scupper's run-off to fall onto a river-washed stone splash box, or add a separate collector box and downspout for the collection of water coming out of the secondary scupper. Water standing on stairs as a result of poor run-off control could open liability questions if someone were to slip and fall.

Design Principle Coordinate all building design areas.

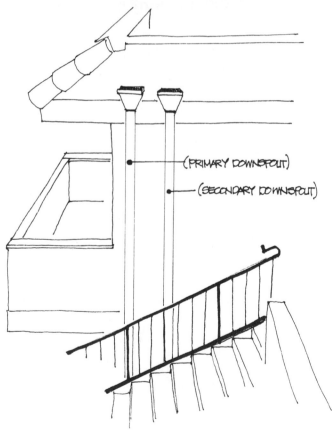

(PRIMARY DOWNSPOUT)

(SECONDARY DOWNSPOUT)

Overflow scupper is missing

Observation   The scupper in the corner of a building's roof presently drains the water adequately. No ponding is occurring around the outlet, and water flows easily to the low point of the roof at the scupper's location. The next nearest drain, however, is completely on the other side of the roof and offers no drainage assistance were this particular scupper to become blocked.

Recommendation   A secondary or overflow scupper should be installed in order to provide a back-up drainage for this corner of the roof. If water were to be prevented from escaping through the present scupper and start ponding, it would add 5 lb. per square foot for every 1" in depth.

Either a roof drain with a sump pan could be added, making it the primary source of drainage, or another scupper could be added to either wall as an ancillary drain. If the latter is the case, the low point of the new scupper should be installed 2" above the low point of the original scupper, with the sizes being identical. If a drain is added, it should have its own drain line, separate from the original drain line, if there is one. The primary line and the secondary line must always drain individually.

Design Principle   Provide a back-up drainage capability when possible.

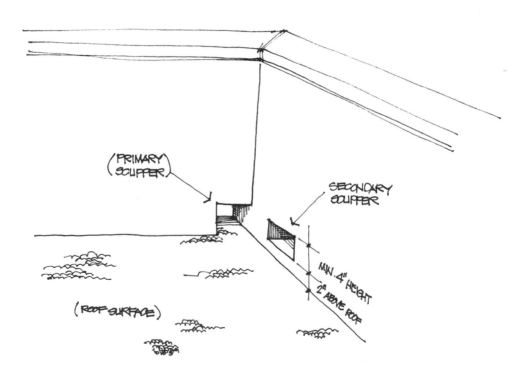

(PRIMARY SCUPPER)

SECONDARY SCUPPER

MIN. 4" HEIGHT

2" ABOVE ROOF

(ROOF SURFACE)

Shingles are cracked along edge

Observation Fractures have been discovered along the end of a sloping shingle roof section, possibly allowing water entry below. Shingles were folded double and fastened with regular roofing nails into the substrate.

Recommendation Sheet metal should have been used along the edge by installing the vertical (side) shingles first, metal along the edge, with a 4" flange, and finally installing the shingles on the sloped section with a ½" overhang on the outside row of shingles.

Shingles should never be folded any more than 45°, the same as any other bituminous sheet roofing (or flashing) material. This goes for both inside and outside corners.

Also, fasteners should never be allowed without counterflashing over their point of entry. A dab of caulking does not qualify as proper counterflashing, contrary to an abundance of existing roofing installations.

Design Principle Reinforce all edges and changes of planes.

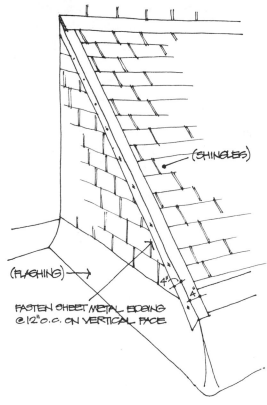

(SHINGLES)

(FLASHING) →

4"

4"

FASTEN SHEET METAL EDGING
@ 12" O.C. ON VERTICAL FACE

Shingles are overexposed

Observation Composition asphalt shingles have been installed in an errant manner, allowing more of the shingle to show than the manufacturer recommends. Now if wind blows the lower shingles up, they could possibly begin to split at the end of the joint between tabs, thus allowing water entry behind the top of the shingle on the row below.

Recommendation Specifications should call for exposure between 5" and 5½" or as manufacturer suggests for nontraditional-shaped shingles. Shingles in this problem case should be removed and replaced, keeping a closer watch on quality control during installation.

Design Principle Refer to manufacturer's recommendations in your specifications, along with dimensions on details.

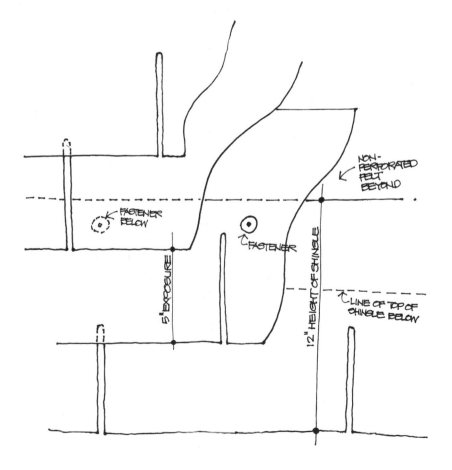

FASTENER BELOW

FASTENER

5" EXPOSURE

12" HEIGHT OF SHINGLE

NON-PERFORATED FELT BEYOND

LINE OF TOP OF SHINGLE BELOW

67

Shingles were specified in high wind situation

Observation Shingles had blown off of a three-year-old building in a location known to experience rather frequent and strong windstorms. A 5' high parapet wall was a contributor to the vortex effect experienced by the shingles, as wind swirled over the wall and up the inside face covered by the shingles. The shingles were not individually tabbed or cemented, so they tore around the staples holding them into place.

Recommendation If shingles are desired by the specifier in a high-wind area, it is best to see to it that each shingle is held into place by both mechanical fastening and adhesion. Cap nails that are hand-nailed will give more holding power than a mechanically-fastened staple system. Plus the tab of each shingle should be pressed into place with a minimum 1" diameter dab of roofing cement or mastic. This is the best prevention to the edge being affected by winds, thereby relieving the fastening of being the sole provider of securement for the shingles.

Design Principle Concern yourself with all surrounding design factors when selecting methods and materials on your roof.

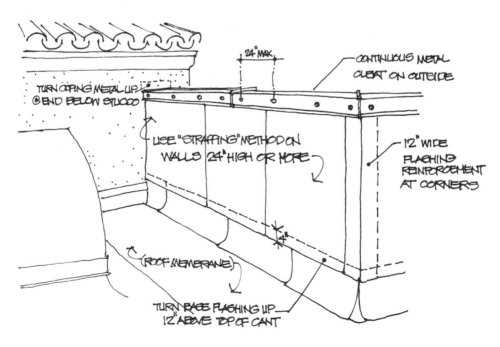

24" MAX

CONTINUOUS METAL
CLEAT ON OUTSIDE

TURN COPING METAL UP
@ END BELOW STUCCO

USE "STRAPPING" METHOD ON
WALLS 24" HIGH OR MORE

12" WIDE
FLASHING
REINFORCEMENT
AT CORNERS

4"

(ROOF MEMBRANE)

TURN BASE FLASHING UP
12" ABOVE TOP OF CANT

Asphalt shingles are pulling around staples

Observation   Shingles had blown off a parapet wall when a wind vortex created by the height of the wall curled up the loose tabs and tore the shingles from around the staples holding them into place.

Recommendation   Two items here need attention. The fastening should have been specified as hand-nailing with 1" diameter cap nails. Mechanically-fastened staples can vary with the amount of penetration. Too little does not hold the shingle in place. Too much digs into the shingle, allowing for easy tearing with the least pressure.

The other item is to specify that each tab on the shingle is spot-adhered with roofing cement. Self-tabbing shingles work adequately on a sloped roof, but, in this case, the wall was completely vertical and the self-sealing did not occur because the shingles never rested on the next one below.

Design Principle   Building cheap can sometimes cost more in the long run than building right.

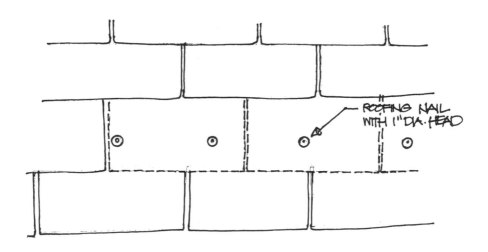

ROOFING NAIL
WITH 1" DIA. HEAD

69

Precariously placed rake tile

Observation Heavy (10-lb.) clay tile along the rake poses a possible hazard to the pedestrians walking below. Double-nailing, as called for in almost all building codes, may not be enough. Nails can back out with time, loosening tile from a previously secure condition.

Unless a different design can be used, safety should take a precedent over appearance when confronted with this predicament. Either the steps should be moved farther away from the wall with the rake tiles above, or a "safety-net" design should be incorporated into the edge along the top, ensuring that any loose tiles will not pose a potential hazard to people below.

Recommendation If pedestrian traffic occurs below, rake tiles should be affixed to the structure incorporating wire ties, along with the minimum double-fastening using screw-type fasteners, to ensure stability.

Design Principle Make safety an integral part of the design phase.

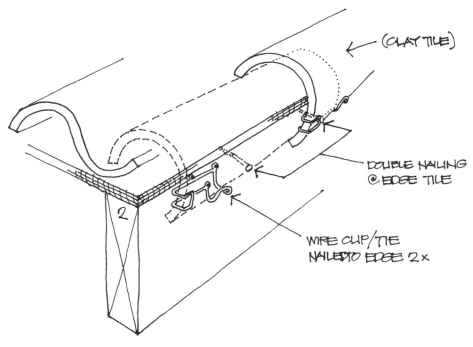

(CLAY TILE)

DOUBLE NAILING
@ EDGE TILE

WIRE CLIP/TIE
NAILED TO EDGE 2×

70

Tiles are broken at corner of roof

Observation   The roofing contractor who installed the clay tile on this project broke the tiles off in areas where whole tiles were not needed, thus allowing open areas and increasing the chances of leaking. No sheet metal was used underneath as a back-up for any openings in the tile work.

Recommendation   Any tiles broken during installation should be removed and replaced with tiles that are cut to fit with a tile saw. Not only does the roofing system work better, it also looks better.

Architects should specify that any tiles requiring less than full size should never be broken, but only saw-cut to fit.

Design Principle   Specify tiles to be saw-cut only. No broken tiles are to be allowed.

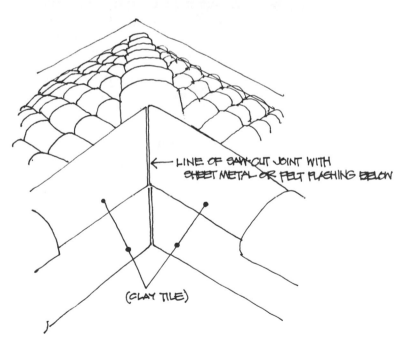

← LINE OF SAW-CUT JOINT WITH
SHEET METAL OR FELT FLASHING BELOW

(CLAY TILE)

End of tile coping was left open

Observation
A termination condition was not addressed in the architect's drawings, leaving the decision open to the field workers on how to finish off the end of a tile coping. As it is now, the end of the coping is open to possible water intrusion, with no means to stop it. The adjacent metal coping also dies out at the end, leaving its termination in the same undecided condition.

Recommendation
The wall topped off with the metal coping should have been raised enough to give the tile coping a termination plane to butt in to. This way the wall below the tile can be flashed into the now higher wall and simply capped off with the tile coping. The metal coping can terminate by itself, without having to involve any other materials.

Design Principle
Design flashing details at the juncture of dissimilar materials.

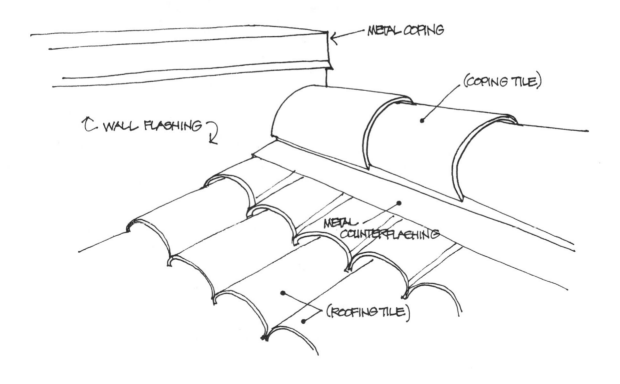

METAL COPING

(COPING TILE)

↰ WALL FLASHING ↲

METAL COUNTERFLASHING

(ROOFING TILE)

Falling concrete tile

Observation   An apartment building had a mansard roof that was covered along the outside edge with a concrete tile system. It was noted, however, in more than one place, that the tiles had become dislodged and were about to fall. Even though the tiles were installed over one-by-two wood batten strips for security, the nails holding the battens to their substrate were being pulled out by the weight of the (10-lb.) concrete tiles. This became a severe liability problem for the apartment owner, since there was constant pedestrian traffic below by the tenants and their guests.

Recommendation   As an architect, keep in mind that form should follow function. In that respect, if the function of the concrete tile is to afford long-lasting water entry protection to the outside of the building, then the form should be secured so as not to endanger someone's health and safety, let alone expose you and your firm to unwanted liability cases in a court of law.

A simple wire tie would be sufficient to hold each tile in place and not affect the desired architectural effect. One step toward a more secure substrate would have been to specify that both the tiles and their batten strips be installed with wood screws to lessen the chance of fasteners backing out.

Design Principle   Make safety an integral part of the design phase.

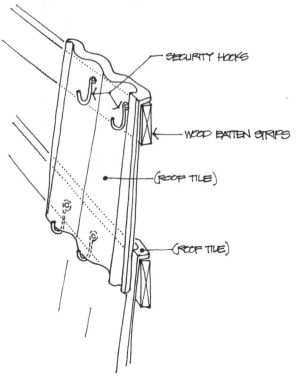

SECURITY HOOKS

WOOD BATTEN STRIPS

(ROOF TILE)

(ROOF TILE)

73

Plywood deck was not blocked

Observation During the removal of an existing faulty roofing system, it was discovered that one of the major contributors to the failure of the roof was the fact that differential movement had occurred between adjacent pieces of plywood decking. This vertical movement, which usually happened during pedestrian or maintenance traffic, caused a shearing motion of the plies of roofing—something that built-up roofing will not tolerate.

Recommendation All joints of the roof decking, no matter the material, must be stabilized so as to remain planar and support the roofing envelope above in a monolithic fashion. In this case, this is achieved by installing wood blocking beneath the transverse (short-dimension) joints in the plywood. The longitudinal (long-dimension) joints are usually centered atop the glu-lam beams or trusses. This way the whole roof deck can act in one plane as a solid base for the desired roofing system.

Design Principle Block edges of plywood decking and mechanically fasten the edges of metal decking for stability.

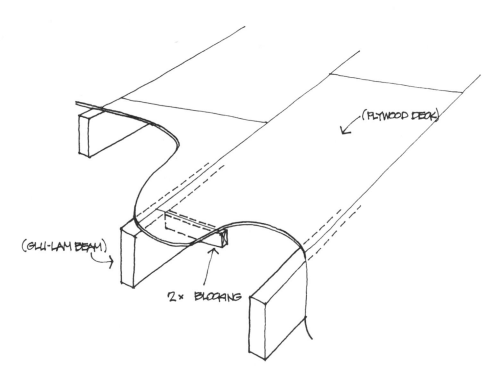

(PLYWOOD DECK)

(GLU-LAM BEAM)

2 × BLOCKING

Roof tears along uneven deck

Observation A fracture in a built-up roof was noted as occurring over an intersection of three pieces of plywood decking. The roofing membrane had split in a **T** shape directly over the deck joints below. On lifting up the roofing, one could see that an 18d common nail had been used to nail the deck to a glu-lam beam and had begun to back out, contributing to the problem. The membrane had sheared in two, however, due to the fact that the decking was not fastened securely and was now in three different planes. Consequently, the roofing membrane, when stepped on, could not handle the differential movement, and the felts simply separated along that axis.

Recommendation Since it makes no sense to install a good roofing system over a questionable deck, the architect must ensure that the deck, once in place, stays in place. This can be accomplished by specifying screw-type fasteners for both plywood and metal decks. Nails are quicker and cheaper on a plywood deck, but constantly threaten the roofing system directly above with the possibility of nails backing out. Spot-welding on a metal deck is, likewise, quicker and cheaper as opposed to deck fasteners, but spot welds are at the mercy of the welder and have been known to fail due to too much or too little welding.

Design Principle Specify items to provide a solid substrate for roofing.

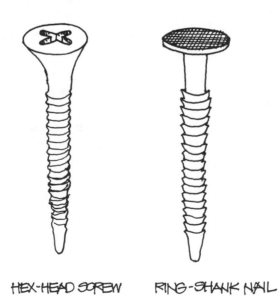

HEX-HEAD SCREW   RING-SHANK NAIL

Roofing membrane is splitting at inside corner of building

Observation The roofing membrane is fracturing along the axis of continuation of the adjacent wall, where the parapet turns. Differential movement is occurring between proximate roof areas and consequently splitting the roofing plies.

The roof is possibly subject to shear and/or tension, depending on the deck type and configuration below.

Recommendation Install control joint along the line of the split, separating the two adjacent roof areas and enabling them to move individually as they require. Each roof area must, and will, act on an independent basis according to its inherent construction assembly. The control joint should have the bellows-type cover fastened on both sides and flashed in to the roof membrane properly. Keeping a low overall profile will lessen the chances of ponding water or restricting proper water flow.

Design Principle Allow for building movement in designing the roof.

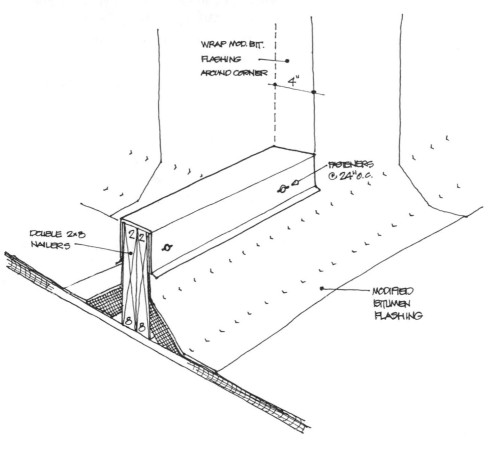

WRAP MOD. BIT.
FLASHING
AROUND CORNER

4"

FASTENERS
@ 24" O.C.

DOUBLE 2x8
NAILERS

2 2

8 8

MODIFIED
BITUMEN
FLASHING

Expansion joint cover blows off

Observation The sheet metal cover over a rather large roof expansion joint has blown off numerous times, exposing the building below to possible water intrusion. The present method of installation is for the outside flanges of the cover to simply hook over each edge of the sheet metal receivers below. While allowing the freedom of movement required, it nonetheless fails because it is not watertight.

Recommendation Increase the gauge thickness of the cover, still keeping with the same type of sheet metal, increase the flange/overlap dimension on each side, and most importantly, fasten the flange on the prevalent windward side into place. This will secure against the chance of blowing off and still allow unrestricted freedom of movement.

Design Principle Refer to NRCA manual for typical roofing details. Don't re-invent the wheel.

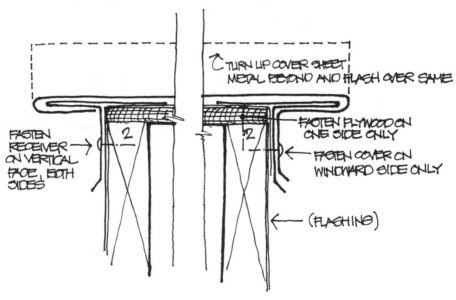

TURN UP COVER SHEET METAL BEYOND AND FLASH OVER SAME

FASTEN RECEIVER ON VERTICAL FACE, BOTH SIDES

FASTEN PLYWOOD ON ONE SIDE ONLY

FASTEN COVER ON WINDWARD SIDE ONLY

(FLASHING)

Expansion joint is not continuous at coping

Observation A wall was noted as having an expansion joint, but it was not noted as being carried through the metal coping that capped the wall. This can only be a source of trouble in the future, because the wall will move, as the expansion joint was designed, but the metal above has been fastened into place and will not allow the kind of movement associated with building expansion.

Recommendation Transfer the expansion joint up through the top of the wall by installing a cover plate over an expansion joint in the metal coping. This way the adjacent pieces of metal can move freely back and forth, protecting the wall from water entry at the same time.

Also, the wall below should have been moved over to where the expansion joint continued from the base of the perpendicular wall, up the wall adjacent to the lower parapet wall, and then up the main wall as is now the case.

Design Principle Don't let expansion joints dead-end into the building.

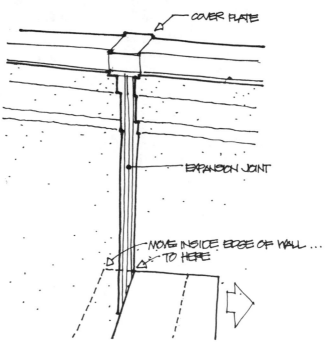

COVER PLATE

EXPANSION JOINT

MOVE INSIDE EDGE OF WALL ...
TO HERE

78

Conduit was fastened through counterflashing

Observation The architect's drawings did not address how to handle rooftop appurtenances, so field laborers attached PVC conduit into the nearest wall penetrating the counterflashing with fasteners. This both increases the chances of a leak at the wall, and makes re-roofing or repairing wall flashing more difficult because of the permanency of the mounting methods used.

Recommendation The conduit is best secured by mounting it on a pressure-treated (or redwood) two-by-four, laying on the roof surface over an extra piece of flashing material. This way it is not permanently attached and can be moved easily, and there is nothing actually penetrating the roof membrane or its flashing, thereby keeping the watertight integrity of the roof intact.

Design Principle Use standard roofing details when conditions permit.

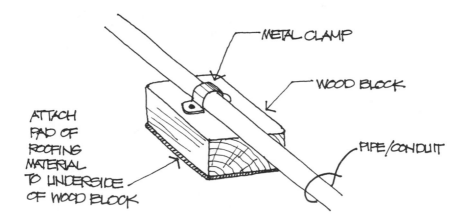

METAL CLAMP

WOOD BLOCK

PIPE/CONDUIT

ATTACH
PAD OF
ROOFING
MATERIAL
TO UNDERSIDE
OF WOOD BLOCK

Refrigerant lines are too close to roof

Observation	Copper refrigerant lines carrying freon to an HVAC unit were noted as being elevated, however minimally, above a roof. Maintenance and re-roofing will be difficult due to lack of proper access to the roof area below.
Recommendation	Of course, it is best to keep this type of condition off of a roof if at all possible, but when it must be done, all pipe runs should be kept up off of the roof a minimum of 24" so that ample space can be afforded to the workers doing the installation or repairs. Resting these supports on the roof is best to allow for movement and to keep from penetrating the roofing membrane.
Design Principle	Design a roof for maintenance and replacement.

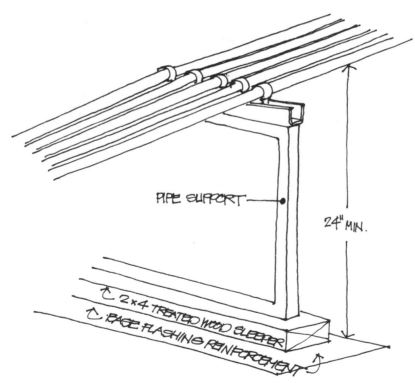

PIPE SUPPORT

24" MIN.

2 x 4 TREATED WOOD SLEEPER

BASE FLASHING REINFORCEMENT

Cracks in pitch pocket filler

Observation A rather large (four foot by six foot) pitch pan was observed to be deteriorating to the point that sizeable cracks were allowing water to enter the building near the penetrations housed within the pitch pocket. The walls of the pitch pan were so flimsy that they had collapsed in two locations, allowing the asphalt-based filler to begin to escape and migrate onto the roof surface.

Recommendation Rather than asking such an oversized pitch pocket to do the work, the specifier should have first mounted the electrical control boxes on a vertical surface so they would remain secure and watertight. A two inch by 12 inch curb covered with flashing and sheet metal would easily remain stationary and secure against water entry.

If that is not used, then a mounting device other than what is now in place (a perforated metal angle) would be much easier to flash, such as a round pipe support. This could be wrapped in flashing, instead of having to rely on a pitch pocket.

Design Principle Use pitch pockets when other methods of flashing are not possible. They are a maintenance item and must be monitored regularly. Too many times they are not.

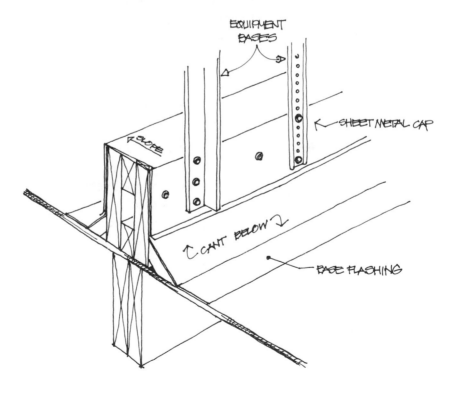

EQUIPMENT BASES

SLOPE

SHEET METAL CAP

CANT BELOW

BASE FLASHING

Angle irons are hard to flash

Observation A new building had a rather high front wall that the architect wanted to brace with supports mounted on the roof. However, his method of support is doomed to constant maintenance and leak calls due to the method of securing the structural member to the building—by welding back-to-back angle irons to the substrate. This, in itself, is not so bad except that these have to go through the roof and somehow be flashed to prevent water intrusion.

The way they were installed will only lead to failure, due to the fact that one cannot properly seal the small gap between the adjacent legs of the angle irons.

Recommendation All that was needed to make this penetration watertight was simply to select a structural shape that was more adept to flashing. In this case, a circular steel shape could have been used in lieu of the angles and then wrapped in flashing material where it penetrated the roof. Anytime you can get away from relying on pitch pockets to keep water out, the longer the roof will last.

Design Principle Don't design-in problems with the roof penetration details.

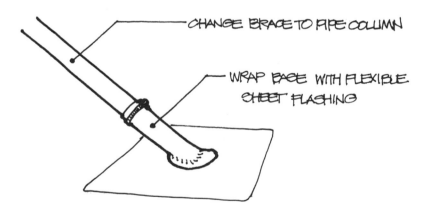

CHANGE BRACE TO PIPE COLUMN

WRAP BASE WITH FLEXIBLE SHEET FLASHING

PART II

Applications

The following pages illustrate examples of good roofing practices, whether they came about in the original design and construction or were incorporated during a re-roof or repair scenario. These examples are also witness to the fact that a roof functioning successfully, due to proper design and construction, does not cost, in essence, any more than one that fails.

82

Sheet metal coping

Explanation Metal coping has been installed along the top of a wall with proper slope toward the interior, seaming technique, and securement.

The slope was achieved by placing a piece of blocking on the outer edge of the wall below the treated wood nailer. This affords protection for the metal coping in case someone steps on it by providing a solid wood base directly below the coping.

The seaming method used was the flat-lock system that ensures against water entry, and yet allows for differential movement between pieces of coping and their substrate.

The fastening was done with a clip on the outside edge of the coping and hex-head screws with neoprene washers on the inside.

Waterproofing of the concrete masonry block came last, with an emulsion spray and aluminum coating.

83

Coping termination at level change

Explanation   The width and height of a parapet wall changed as part of an architectural element along a roof edge. What usually happens at the end of the metal coping on the lower wall is simply to butt it into the higher wall and smear mastic on the open edge. This never works.

In this case, the lower coping turns up the wall high enough to be counterflashed by the higher wall's metal. Then the wall flashing below the coping continues along the wall and is terminated at the top with a two-piece counterflashing. This type of counterflashing allows removal of the metal for repair or replacement. Note the manner in which the wall flashing is installed—in workable sizes and in a neat and orderly fashion.

Proper coping treatment at wall change

Explanation   A pilaster occurring along the outside of a parapet wall extends up to the top of the wall and has to be included in the coverage by the sheet metal coping. Note that the coping has a standing-seam joint at each side of the area where the wall increases in thickness. This is where the differential movement will be concentrated and, consequently, where the coping needs the most attention to combat this movement. The coping is then fastened at 24" intervals along the inside.

Roof access ladder

Explanation A ladder is mounted on a parapet wall after application of wall flashing so that the penetration made by the fasteners is protected against water entry.

Keeping the penetrations through the plane of the roof at a minimum is one easy way to reduce the chance of roof leaks. Whenever possible, move or change the design of a penetration so that the possibility of causing a leak is virtually eliminated.

Wall treatment

Explanation A parapet wall is flashed with techniques employing good roofing practice—virtually maintenance-free coping on top of the wall flashing that protects the top and side of the wall, sending the water during a rainstorm down onto the roof for drainage.

In reverse water-flow direction, the roofing plies are turned up over the cant at the perimeter, putting the edge of the roofing membrane up out of the plane of standing water. Next, a base sheet is installed to cover where the plies are nailed off, using a flexible membrane (modified bitumen in this case) to handle any incremental movement where a change of planes occurs. Then, in shingle fashion, the modified bitumen wall treatment laps the base flashing 4" along the bottom edge and continues up and over the outside edge of the wall before fastening at 6" o. c.

Then, when the coping is installed, a clip (either intermediate or continuous, depending on the local wind conditions) is installed along the outer edge of the nailer, hooking the coping over the clip and fastening off the coping along the inside edge with removeable fasteners and neoprene washers. This type of fastener protects against water entry at the point of penetration through the metal coping and allows for removal of the coping, when necessary.

Wall flashing

Explanation   A knee wall on the roof has been flashed and is now awaiting sheet metal coping to be installed along the top. Note that the base flashing was installed first over the plies and the cant, and then the wall flashing was lapped over the top of the base flashing and around the corners. Then the laps were sealed and the top of the flashing was mechanically fastened at 4" o. c.

88

Sheet metal cap on roof curb

Explanation   A curb for a rooftop mechanical unit was capped off with sheet metal that was too large to do in one piece. The seaming method used for the two pieces of sheet metal was a standing seam. This allows for a watertight seal along the joint between the metal sheets and helps to stiffen the metal against possible pedestrian roof traffic. Fastening was done later along the outer vertical edge to facilitate removal during maintenance and to prevent water entry within the curb.

Rooftop fan curbs

Explanation   An architect called out in the specifications for all roof penetrations to be at least 24" apart, and then saw it through to reality by coordinating the mechanical plan into the roof plan and made sure the curbs were built far enough apart to allow proper flashing. The result was two independent roof curbs that can now function without the threat of water intrusion. Also note the height of the curbs, well above the 8" minimum height called for in the specs and the securement done in the vertical plane on the outside edge of the metal cap.

90

Curb flashing

Explanation   Modified bitumen flashing was installed on a roof curb prior to the installation of the sheet metal cap, as the rational sequence would demand. Note that the flashing turns over the top of the wood curb and is mechanically fastened with cap nails on 12" centers along the horizontal plane. When the metal cap is put on, the fasteners for it will go on the vertical metal surface and through the flashing. The flashing will then, in turn, seal around the cap fasteners, providing a watertight condition.

Note, also, the flashing height of both curbs and their distance apart.

91

Vent stack flashing

Explanation A lead boot was properly installed over a vent pipe. The flange was set in a bed of mastic and nailed along the outer edge. Then the whole boot was "sandwiched" into the roofing system using the proper roofing techniques. This particular pipe had the lead turned down into the pipe. The other way is to install a lead cap over the pipe. Either way is acceptable and will offer years of maintenance-free performance.

Wall flashing at chimney

Explanation   A parapet wall with tile coping butts into a
brick chimney. Flashing is made difficult due
to the rough nature of the brick and the gaps
caused by the joints between masonry units.
The solution shown here has provided a
watertight connection due to proper flashing
methods.

The counterflashing at the bottom of the chimney has been saw-cut into the brick high
enough up from the roof surface to eliminate
the danger of ponded water causing a problem.

Both the tile coping and the wall flashing have
been terminated into a piece of sheet metal that
was installed first in a bed of roofing cement
and mechanically fastened into the brick to
provide an even seal of protection at the change
of planes. Then caulking was applied along the
edge to reinforce the water entry protection.

Overflow scupper

Explanation   Roof drains along the outer edge of a building carry all of the water flowing off the roof during rainstorms into roof drains. The decision was made to have a few large roof drains as opposed to having more, smaller drains to cut down on plumbing costs.

This makes the Uniform Building Code requirement for overflow drainage ever more valuable. If one of the few drains were to become clogged and start causing water to back up, ponding will occur quicker than one drain out of many. The 2" height for an overflow stems from the weight of water, 5 lb. per square foot for every 1" depth, to only reach 10 lb. per square foot at a clogged drain prior to the activation of an overflow. Almost any building should be able to handle 10 lb. per square foot in extra loading without taxing its structural system.

Smooth-surface roof

Explanation The roof on a shopping center was re-roofed with a smooth-surface built-up roof. Note good positive slope, ample height on all curbs, vent pipes flashed with lead boots, and the continuation of the monolithic surface coating up the parapet walls, pipes, and curbs.

The roofing system affords protection for the interior against possible water entry, while at the same time making it easier to find the source of leaks for repairs. This, in turn, is protected by the coating, which is re-applied every few years, depending on the amount of coating installed originally and the local weather conditions. It is easier to maintain the coating than it is to maintain the roof.

Cricket along high roof

Explanation   A water diverter was designed into a roofing system that had the main drainage along a central spline down the middle of the roof. The large raised roof section was centered over this drain line, so the architect saw to it that the two outside walls of the high roof, parallel to the drain line and perpendicular to the water flow, were able to kick the water toward the drains in a positive manner. This was accomplished by building up the roof deck prior to roofing with a cricket that sent the water to one end of the roof or the other. Roof drains were then installed on each side of the high roof in the central valley of the roof.

Proper roof drainage

Explanation   A commercial building's roof was designed practically void of curbs and penetrations. The architect had the foresight to group all mechanical units together in just a few locations, freeing up the roof to drain water easily. So, along with a smooth-surface roof having positive slope to the drains, there is little chance of standing water.

The overflow scupper in the background, located on the parapet wall behind the roof drain, is properly installed to assist drainage in case the primary drain ceases to function.

Positive roof drainage

Explanation This roof drains mainly along a valley that runs down the middle of the roof. But within the valley, and between each of the roof drains, is a cricket system that provides positive drainage to the drains and keeps water from ponding at the low points. This can be achieved by building up either insulation or plywood prior to the installation of the roofing system. As a designer, remember to double the slope of the crickets to overcome the slope of the roof in the valley. For example, if the slope of the roof is ¼" per foot, you would have to make the cricket's slope ½" per foot. Otherwise, in using the same slope, you only break even and wind up with a dead-level roof.

Mechanical unit support

Explanation   A massive air-conditioning system was installed on a roof that required structural support. Rather than sitting it on **I**-beams welded to the steel deck below and then trying to roof around it, or running an **H**-shaped column up through the roof and trying to seal it with a pitch pocket, the simple approach was used in the design.

A circular steel column was welded to the structural system at the deck level, and welded to a **U**-shaped strap that held a solid wood member supporting the whole HVAC unit. Then the flashing for the column was done rather easily by treating it as a vent pipe and using lead flashing and a compression ring around the top.

99

Pipe support protection

Explanation   This large pipe was elevated off the finished
roof surface and had to be treated so that it was
both supported and free to move in a linear
fashion as the fluids inside demanded. The
metal support keeps the pipe up off the roof,
and the roof is protected from the possible
movement of the support with two items—a
wood nailer attached to the support and a piece
of modified bitumen installed between the
wood and the roof. Note that the clamp on the
support allows the pipe freedom of movement
as necessary.

100

Ganged-pipe flashing

Explanation   A number of pipes penetrated the roof, so the architect simply had a number of them go through the roof in one place and protected the hole made by the pipes with a rain hood. Now, not only is the interior protected from water entry by a maintenance-free flashing detail, but the pipes are free to move as the temperature of the fluids in the pipes fluctuates. This eliminates the chance of the flashing around a pipe breaking loose.

Note the curb height of the flashing cap.

Proper mechanical support

Explanation   The steel angles that support the rather large mechanical duct do not penetrate the roof, but do terminate at roof level. Rather than have them rest on a metal base at the finished roof surface, the architect provided a detail that showed the angle's metal base should rest not only on a treated 2″ thick wood sleeper, but should also have an extra piece of modified bitumen between the wood and the finished roof surface. This would add little extra cost, if any, to the project, yet afford a lifetime of maintenance-free protection of the roof at each location of the metal angles.

Glossary*

Aggregate (1) crushed stone, crushed slag or water worn gravel used for surfacing a built-up roof; (2) any granular mineral material.

Alligatoring the cracking of the surfacing bitumen on a built-up roof, producing a pattern of cracks similar to an alligator's hide; the cracks may or may not extend through the surfacing bitumen .

Application Rate the quantity (mass, volume or thickness) of material applied per unit area.

Area Divider a raised, double wood member attached to a properly flashed wood base plate that is anchored to the roof deck. It is used to relieve thermal stresses in a roof system where no expansion joints have been provided. (See NRCA Construction Details.)

Asbestos a group of natural, fibrous, impure silicate materials.

Asphalt a dark brown to black cementitious material in which the predominating constituents are bitumens, which occur in nature or are obtained in petroleum processing.

Dead-Level Asphalt a roofing asphalt conforming to the requirements of ASTM Specification D312, Type 1.

Flat Asphalt a roofing asphalt conforming to the requirements of ASTM Specification D312, Type 11.

* Reprinted by permission of the National Roofing Contractors Association.

Steep Asphalt   a roofing asphalt conforming to the requirements of ASTM Specification D312, Type 111.

Special Steep Asphalt   a roofing asphalt conforming to the requirements of ASTM Specification D312, Type IV.

Asphalt, Air Blown   an asphalt produced by blowing air through molten asphalt at an elevated temperature to raise its softening point and modify other properties.

Asphalt Felt   an asphalt-saturated felt or an asphalt coated felt.

Asphalt Mastic   a mixture of asphaltic material and graded mineral aggregate that can be poured when heated but requires mechanical manipulation to apply when cool.

Asphalt, Steam Blown   an asphalt produced by blowing steam through molten asphalt to modify its properties.

Asphaltene   a high molecular weight hydrocarbon fraction precipitated from asphalt by a designated paraffinic naphtha solvent at a specified temperature and solvent-asphalt ratio.
NOTE—The asphaltene fraction should be identified by the temperature and solvent asphalt ratio used.

Backnailing   the practice of blind-nailing roofing felts to a substrate in addition to hot-mopping to prevent slippage. (See Blind Nailing.)

Base Flashing   (See Flashing)

Base Ply   the lowermost ply of roofing material in a roof membrane assembly.

Base Sheet   a saturated or coated felt placed as the first ply in some multi-ply built-up roof membranes.

Bitumen (1) a class of amorphous, black or dark colored, (solid, semi-solid or viscous) cementitious substances, natural or manufactured, composed principally of high molecular weight hydrocarbons, soluble in carbon disulfide, and found in asphalts, tars, pitches and asphaltites; (2) a generic term used to denote any material composed principally of bitumen.

Bituminous containing or treated with bitumen. Examples: bituminous concrete, bituminous felts and fabrics, bituminous pavement.

Bituminous Emulsion (1) a suspension of minute globules of bituminous material in water or in an aqueous solution; (2) a suspension of minute globules of water or an aqueous solution in a liquid bituminous material (invert emulsion).

Bituminous Grout a mixture of bituminous material and fine sand that will flow into place without mechanical manipulation when heated.

Blackberry a small bubble or blister in the flood coating of a gravel-surfaced roof membrane.

Blind Nailing the practice of nailing the back portion of a roofing ply in a manner that the fasteners are not exposed to the weather in the finished product.

Blister an enclosed pocket of air mixed with water or solvent vapor, trapped between impermeable layers of felt, or between the felt and substrate.

Blocking wood built into a roofing system above the deck and below the membrane and flashing to stiffen the deck around an opening, act as a stop for insulation, or to serve as a nailer for attachment of the membrane or flashing.

Bond the adhesive and cohesive forces holding two roofing components in intimate contact.

Brooming embedding a ply of roofing material by using a broom to smooth out the ply and ensure contact with the adhesive under the ply.

British Thermal Unit (Btu) the heat energy required to raise the temperature of 1 pound of water 1 degree Fahrenheit.

Built-Up Roof Membrane a continuous, semi-flexible roof membrane assembly, consisting of plies of saturated felts, coated felts, fabrics or mats between which alternate layers of bitumen are applied, generally surfaced with mineral aggregate, bituminous materials, or a granule-surfaced roofing sheet. (Abbreviation: BUR.)

Cant Strip a beveled strip used under flashing to modify the angle at the point where the roofing or waterproofing membrane meets any vertical element.

Cap Flashing (See Flashing.)

Capillarity the action by which the surface of a liquid (where it is in contact with a solid) is elevated or depressed, depending upon the relative attraction of the molecules of the liquid for each other and for those of the solid.

Cap Sheet a granule-surfaced coated sheet used as the top ply of a built-up roof membrane or flashing.

Caulking a composition of vehicle and pigment, used at ambient temperatures for filling joints, that remains plastic for an extended time after application.

Coal Tar a dark brown to black, semi-solid hydrocarbon obtained as residue from the partial evaporation or distillation of coal tar.

Coal-Tar Pitch   a coal tar used as the waterproofing agent in dead-level or low slope built-up roof membrane, conforming to ASTM Specification D450, Type 1.

Coal-Tar Waterproofing Pitch   a coal tar used as the dampproofing or waterproofing agent in below-grade structures, conforming to ASTM Specification D450, Type 11.

Coal-Tar Bitumen   a coal tar used as the waterproofing agent in dead-level or low slope built-up roof membrane, conforming to ASTM D450, Type 111.

Coal-Tar Felts   a felt that has been saturated with refined coal tar.

Coated Sheet Felt   (1) an asphalt felt that has been coated on both sides with harder, more viscous asphalt; (2) a glass fiber felt that has been simultaneously impregnated and coated with asphalt on both sides.

Cold-Processing Roofing   a continuous, semi-flexible roof membrane, consisting of plies of felts, mats or fabrics that are laminated on a roof with alternate layers of cold-applied roof cement and surfaced with a cold-applied coating.

Condensation   the conversion of water vapor or other gas to liquid as the temperature drops or the atmospheric pressure rises. (See Dew-Point.)

Coping   the covering piece on top of a wall exposed to the weather, usually sloped to shed water.

Counterflashing   formed metal or elastomeric sheeting secured on or into a wall, curb, pipe, rooftop unit or other surface, to cover and protect the upper edge of a base flashing and its associated fasteners.

Course	(1) the term used for each application of material that forms the waterproofing system or the flashing; (2) one layer of a series of materials applied to a surface (i.e., a five-course wall flashing is composed of three applications of mastic with one ply of felt sandwiched between each layer of mastic).
Coverage	the surface area continuously covered by a specific quantity of a particular roofing material.
Crack	a separation or fracture occurring in a roof membrane or roof deck, generally caused by thermal induced stress or substrate movement.
Creep	the permanent deformation of a roofing material or roof system caused by the movement of the roof membrane that results from continuous thermal stress or loading.
Cricket	a relatively small, elevated area of a roof constructed to divert water around a chimney, curb or other projection.
Cutback	solvent-thinned bitumen used in cold process roofing adhesives, flashing cements and roof coatings.
Cutoff	a detail designed to prevent lateral water movement into the insulation where the membrane terminates at the end of a day's work, or used to isolate sections of the roofing system. It is usually removed before the continuation of the work.
Dampproofing	treatment of a surface or structure to resist the passage of water in the absence of hydrostatic pressure.
Dead Level	absolutely horizontal, or zero slope. (See Slope.)
Dead-Level Asphalt	(See Asphalt.)

Dead Loads	non-moving rooftop loads, such as mechanical equipment, air conditioning units, and the roof deck itself.
Deck	the structural surface to which the roofing or waterproofing system (including insulation) is applied.
Delamination	separation of the plies in a roof membrane system or separation of laminated layers of insulation .
Dew Point	the temperature at which water vapor starts to condense in cooling air at the existing atmospheric pressure and vapor content.
Double-Pour	the process of applying two layers of aggregate and bitumen to a built-up roof.
Drain	a device that allows for the flow of water from a roof area. (See NRCA Construction Details.)
Dropback	a reduction in the softening point of bitumen that occurs when bitumen is heated in the absence of air. (See Softening Point Drift.)
Edge Sheets	felt strips that are cut to widths narrower than the standard width of the full felt roll, used to start the felt shingling pattern at a roof edge.
Edge Stripping	application of felt strips cut to narrower widths than the normal felt roll width to cover a joint between flashing and built-up roofing.
Edge Venting	the practice of providing regularly spaced protected opening along a roof perimeter to relieve moisture vapor pressure.
Elastomer	a macromolecular material that returns rapidly to its approximate initial dimensions and shape after substantial deformation by a weak stress and the subsequent release of that stress.

Elastomeric a rubber like synthetic polymer that will stretch when pulled and will return quickly to its original shape when released.

Embedment (1) the process of pressing a felt, aggregate, fabric, mat, or panel uniformly and completely into hot bitumen or adhesive; (2) the process of pressing granules into coating in the manufacture of factory prepared roofing.

Emulsion the intimate dispersion of an organic material and water achieved by using a chemical or clay emulsifying agent.

Envelope a continuous membrane edge seal formed at the perimeter and at penetrations by folding the base sheet or ply over the plies above and securing it to the top of the membrane. The envelope prevents bitumen seepage from the edge of the membrane.

Equilibrium Moisture (1) the moisture content of a material stabilized at a given temperature and relative humidity, expressed as percent moisture by weight; (2) the typical moisture content of a material in any given geographical area.

Equiviscous Temperature (EVT) the temperature at which the viscosity is 75 centipoise for asphalt and 25 centipoise for coal tar products; the recommended temperature plus or minus 25 F at the time of application

Expansion Joint a structural separation between two building elements that allows free movement between the elements without damage to the roofing or waterproofing system.

Exposure (1) the traverse dimension of a roofing element not overlapped by an adjacent element in any roof system. The exposure of any ply in a membrane may be computed by dividing the felt width minus 2 inches by the number of shingled plies; thus, the exposure of 36 inch-wide felt in a shingled, four-ply membrane should be 8½ inches; (2) the time during which a portion of a roofing element is exposed to the weather.

Fabric a woven cloth of organic or inorganic filaments, threads or yarns.

Factory Mutual (FM) an organization that classifies roof assemblies for their fire characteristics and wind uplift resistance for insurance companies in the United States.

Factory Square 108 square feet of roofing material.

Fallback (See Dropback.)

Felt a flexible sheet manufactured by the interlocking of fibers through a combination of mechanical work, moisture and heat. Felts are manufactured principally from vegetable fibers (organic felts), asbestos fibers (asbestos felts) or glass fibers (glass fiber felts); other fibers may be present in each type.

Felt Layer a machine used for applying bitumen and built-up roofing felts.

Felt Mill Ream the mass in pounds of 480 square feet of dry, unsaturated felt; also termed "point weight."

Fine Mineral Surfacing water-insoluble, inorganic material, more than 50 percent of which passes the No. 35 sieve, used on the surface of roofing.

Fishmouth (1) a half-cylindrical or half-conical opening formed by an edge wrinkle; (2) in shingles, a half-conical opening formed at a cut edge.

Flashing the system used to seal membrane edges at walls, expansion joints, drains, Gravel stops, and other places where the membrane is interrupted or terminated. Base flashing covers the edge of the membrane. Cap flashing or counterflashing shields the upper edges of the base flashing.

Flashing Cement a trowelable mixture of cutback bitumen and mineral stabilizers, including asbestos or other inorganic fibers.

Flat Asphalt (See Asphalt.)

Flood Coat the top layer of bitumen into which the aggregate is embedded on an aggregate-surfaced built up roof.

Fluid Applied an elastomeric material, fluid at ambient temperature, that dries or cures after application to form a continuous membrane. Such systems normally do not incorporate reinforcement.

Glass Felt glass fibers bonded into a sheet with resin and suitable for impregnation in the manufacture of bituminous waterproofing materials, roof membranes, and shingles.

Glass Mat a thin mat composed of glass fibers with or without a binder.

Glaze Coat (1) the top layer of asphalt in a smooth surfaced built-up roof assembly; (2) a thin protective coating of bitumen applied to the lower plies or top ply of a built up roof membrane when application of additional felts or the flood coat and aggregate surfacing are delayed.

Gravel course, granular aggregate, with pieces larger than sand grains, resulting from the natural erosion of rock.

Gravel Spot	a flanged device, frequently metallic, designed to provide a continuous finished edge for roofing material and to prevent loose aggregate from washing off of the roof.
Headlap	the minimum distance, measured at 90 degrees to the eaves along the face of a shingle or felt, from the upper edge of the shingle or felt to the nearest exposed surface.
Holiday	an area where a liquid-applied material is missing.
"Hot Stuff" or "Hot"	the roofer's term for hot bitumen.
Hygroscopic	attracting, absorbing and retaining atmospheric moisture.
Ice Dam	a mass of ice formed at the transition from a warm to a cold roof surface, frequently formed by refreezing meltwater at the overhang of a steep roof, causing ice and water to back up under roofing materials.
Incline	the slope of a roof expressed either in percent or in the number of vertical units of rise per horizontal unit of run.
Inorganic	being or composed of matter other than hydrocarbons and their derivatives, or matter that is not of plant or animal origin.
Insulation	(See Thermal Insulation.)
Job-Average Basis	a technique for determining the average dimensions or quantities of materials, by analysis of roof test cuts. The technique requires a minimum of three test cuts per roof area, plus one cut for each additional 10,000 square feet of roof area. Job-average basis is computed by dividing the sum of all measurements taken by the

number of measurements taken. The results would describe the job-average for the quantity or dimension.

Knot an imperfection or non-homogeneity in materials used in fabric construction, the presence of which causes surface irregularities.

Live Loads moving roof installation equipment, wind, snow, ice or rain.

Mastic (See Flashing Cement or Asphalt Mastic.)

Membrane a flexible or semi-flexible roof covering or waterproofing layer, whose primary function is the exclusion of water.

Mesh the square opening of a sieve.

Metal Flashing (See Flashing.) Metal flashing is frequently used as through-wall flashing, cap flashing, counterflashing or gravel stops.

Mineral Fiber Felt a felt with mineral wood as its principal component.

Mineral Granules opaque, natural, or synthetically colored aggregate commonly used to surface cap sheets, granule-surfaced sheets, and roofing shingles.

Mineral Stabilizer a fine, water-insoluble inorganic material, used in a mixture with solid or semi-solid bituminous materials.

Mineral-Surfaced Roofing built-up roofing materials whose top ply consists of a granule-surfaced sheet.

Mineral-Surfaced Sheet a felt that is coated on one or both sides with asphalt and surfaced with mineral granules

Modified Bitumen are composite sheets consisting of a copolymer modified bitumen often reinforced and sometimes surfaced with various types of films, foils and mats.

Mole Run   a meandering ridge in a roof membrane not associated with insulation or deck joints.

Mop-and-Flop   an application procedure in which roofing elements (insulation boards, felt plies, cap sheets, etc.) are initially placed upside down adjacent to their ultimate locations, are coated with adhesive, and are then turned over and applied to the substrate.

Mopping   the application of hot bitumen with a mop or mechanical applicator to the substrate or to the felts of a built-up roof membrane.

Solid Mopping   a continuous mopping of a surface, leaving no unmopped areas.

Spot Mopping   a mopping pattern in which hot bitumen is applied in roughly circular areas, leaving a grid of unmopped, perpendicular bands on the roof.

Sprinkle Mopping   a random mopping pattern in which heated bitumen beads are strewn onto the substrate with a brush or mop.

Strip Mopping   a mopping pattern in which hot bitumen is applied in parallel bands.

Neoprene   a synthetic rubber (polychloroprene) used in liquid-applied and sheet-applied elastomeric roof membranes or flashings.

Nineteen-Inch Selvage   a prepared roofing sheet with a 17-inch granule surfaced exposure and a nongranule-surfaced 19-inch selvage edge. This material is sometimes referred to as SIS or as Wide Selvage Asphalt Roll Roofing Material Surfaced with Mineral Granules.

Ninety-Pound	a prepared organic felt roll roofing with a granule surfaced exposure that has a mass of approximately 90 pounds per 100 square feet.
Organic	being or composed of hydrocarbons or their derivatives, or matter of plant or animal origin.
Parapet Wall	that part of any wall entirely above the roof.
Perlite	an aggregate used in lightweight insulating concrete and in preformed perlitic insulation boards, formed by heating and expanding siliceous volcanic glass.
Perm	a unit of water vapor transmission defined as 1 grain of water vapor per square foot per hour per inch of mercury pressure difference (1 inch of mercury = 0.49 psi). The formula for perm is: P = GRAINS OF WATERVAPOR/SQUARE FOOT × HOUR× INCH MERCURY
Permeance	an index of a material's resistance to water vapor transmission. (See Perm.)
Phased Application	the installation of a roof system or water proofing system during two or more separate time intervals.
Picture Framing	a rectangular pattern of ridges in a roof membrane over insulation or deck joints.
Pitch	(See Coal Tar and Incline.)
Pitch Pocket	a flange, open-bottomed, metal container placed around columns or other roof penetrations that is filled with hot bitumen or flashing cement to seal the joint. The use of pitch pockets is not recommended by NRCA.
Plastic Cement	(See Flashing Cement.)
Plastomeric	a plastic like polymer consisting of any of various complex organic compounds produced

by polymerization which are capable of being molded, extruded or cast into various shapes or films. Generally they are thermo plastic in nature, i.e., they will soften when heated and harden when cooled.

Ply   a layer of felt in a built-up roof membrane system. A four-ply membrane system has four plies of felt.

Point Weight   (See Felt Mill Ream.)

Pond   a roof surface that is incompletely drained.

Positive Drainage   the drainage condition in which consideration has been made for all loading deflections of the deck, and additional roof slope has been provided to ensure drainage of the roof area within 48 hours of rainfall.

Primer   a thin, liquid bitumen applied to a surface to improve the adhesion of subsequent applications of bitumen.

Rake   the slope edge of a roof at the first or last rafter.

Re-covering   the process of covering an existing roofing system with a new roofing system.

Re-entrant Corner   an inside corner of a surface, producing stress concentrations in the roofing or waterproofing membrane.

Reglet   a groove in a wall or other surface adjoining a roof surface for use in the attachment of counterflashing.

Reinforced Membrane   a roofing or waterproofing membrane reinforced with felts, mats, fabrics or chopped fibers.

Relative Humidity   the ratio of the weight of moisture in a given volume of air-vapor mixture to the saturated (maximum) weight of water vapor at the same temperature, expressed as a percentage. For example, if the weight of the moist air is 1 pound and if the air could hold 2 pounds of water vapor at a given temperature, the relative humidity (RH) is 50 percent.

Replacement the practice of removing an existing roof system and replacing it with a new roofing system.

Re-roofing the process of re-covering or replacing an existing roofing system. (See Re-covering and Re-placement.)

Ridging an upward, tenting displacement of a roof membrane frequently occurring over insulation joints, deck joints and base sheet edges.

Roll Roofing smooth-surfaced or mineral-surfaced coated felts.

Roof Assembly an assembly of interacting roof components (including the roof deck) designed to weather-proof and, normally, to insulate a building's top surface.

Roof Cement (See Flashing Cement.)

Roofer the trade name for the workman who applied roofing material.

Roof System a system of interacting roof components (not including the roof deck) designed to weather proof and, normally, to insulate a building's top surface.

Saddle a small structure that helps channel surface water to drains, frequently located in a valley, and often constructed like a small hip roof or like a pyramid with a diamond shape base. (See Cricket.)

Saturated Felt a felt that has been partially saturated with low softening point bitumen.

Screen an apparatus with circular apertures for separating sizes of materials.

Scuttle a hatch that provides access to the roof from the interior of the building.

Seal (1) a narrow closure strip made of bituminous materials; (2) to secure a roof from the entry of moisture.

Sealant a mixture of polymers, fillers, and pigments used to fill and seal joints where moderate movement is expected; it cures to a resilient solid.

Selvage an edge or edging that differs from the main part of (1) a fabric, or (2) granule-surfaced roll roofing material.

Selvage Joint a lapped joint designed for mineral-surfaced cap sheets. The mineral surfacing is omitted over a small portion of the longitudinal edge of the sheet below in order to obtain better adhesion of the lapped cap sheet surface with the bituminous adhesive.

Shark Fin an upward-curled felt side lap or end lap.

Shingle (1) a small unit of prepared roofing material designed for installation with similar units in overlapping rows on inclines normally exceeding 25 percent; (2) to cover with shingles; (3) to apply any sheet material in overlapping rows like shingles.

Shingling (1) the procedure of laying parallel felts so that one longitudinal edge of each felt overlaps and the other longitudinal edge underlaps, and adjacent felt. (See Ply.) Normally, felts are shingled on a slope so that the water flows over rather than against each lap; (2) the application of shingles to a sloped roof.

Sieve an apparatus with apertures for separating sizes of material.

Slag a hard, air-cooled aggregate that is left as a residue from blast furnaces, used as a surfacing aggregate.

Slippage relative lateral movement of adjacent components of a built-up membrane. It occurs mainly in roofing membranes on a slope, sometimes exposing the lower plies or even the base sheet to the weather.

Slope (See Incline.)

Smooth-Surfaced Roof a built-up roof membrane surfaced with a layer of hot-mopped asphalt, cold-applied asphalt clay emulsion, cold-applied, asphalt cutback, or sometimes with an unmopped inorganic felt.

Softening Point the temperature at which bitumen becomes soft enough to flow, as determined by an arbitrary, closely defined method.

Softening Point Drift a change in the softening point of bitumen during storage or application. (See Dropback.)

Solid Mopping See Mopping.)

Special Steep Asphalt (See Asphalt.)

Split a membrane tear resulting from tensile strength.

Split Sheet (See Nineteen-Inch Selvage.)

Spot Mopping (See Mopping.)

Sprinkle Mopping (See Mopping.)

Spudding	the process of removing the roofing aggregate and most of the bituminous top coating by scraping and chipping.
Square	the term used to describe 100 square feet of roof area.
Stack Vent	a vertical outlet in a built-up roof system designed to relieve the pressure exerted by moisture vapor between the roof membrane and the vapor retarder or deck.
Steep Asphalt	(See Asphalt.)
Strip Mopping	(See Mopping.)
Stripping or Strip-Flashing	(1) the technique of sealing a joint between metal and the built-up roof membrane with one or two plies of felt or fabric and hot-applied or cold-applied bitumen; (2) the technique of taping joints between insulation boards or deck panels.
Substrate	the surface upon which the roofing or waterproofing membrane is applied (i.e., the structural deck or insulation).
Sump	an intentional depression around a drain.
Superimposed Loads	loads that are added to existing loads. For example, a large stack of insulation boards placed on top of a structural steel deck.
Tapered Edge Strip	a tapered insulation strip used to (1) elevate the roof at the perimeter and at curbs that extend through a roof; (2) provide a gradual transition from one layer of insulation to another.
Taping	(See Stripping.)
Tar	a brown or black bituminous material, liquid or semi-solid in consistency, in which the predominating constituents are bitumens obtained

as condensates in the processing of coal, petro-leum, oil-shale, wood, or other organic materials.

Tarred Felt (See Coal-Tar Felt.)

Test Cut a sample of the roof membrane that is cut from a roof membrane to: (a) determine the weight of the average interply bitumen moppings; (b) diagnose the condition of the exiting membrane (e.g., to detect leaks or blisters).

Thermal Conductance (C) a unit of heat flow that is used for specific thicknesses of material or for materials of combination construction, such as laminated insulation. The formula for thermal conductance is:

$$C = \frac{k}{\text{THICKNES IN INCHES}}$$

Thermal Conductivity (k) the heat energy that will be transmitted by conduction through 1 square foot of 1-inch thick homogeneous material in one hour when there is a difference of 1 degree Fahrenheit perpendicularly across the two surfaces of the material. The formula for thermal conductivity is:

k = Btu/SQUARE FOOT / INCH / HOUR / DEGREE FAHRENHEIT

Thermal Insulation a material applied to reduce the flow of heat.

Thermal Resistance (R) an index of a material's resistance to heat flow; it is the reciprocal of thermal conductivity (k) or thermal conductance (C). The formula for thermal resistance is:

$$R = \frac{1}{C} \text{ or } R = \frac{1}{k} \text{ or } R = \frac{\text{THICKNESS IN INCHES}}{k}$$

Thermal Shock the stress-producing phenomenon resulting from sudden temperature changes in a roof membrane when, for example, a rain shower follows brilliant sunshine.

Through-Wall Flashing	a water-resistant membrane or material assembly extending through a wall and its cavities, positioned to direct water entering the top of the wall to the exterior.
Tuck Pointing	(1) troweling mortar into a joint after masonry units are laid; (2) final treatment of joints in cut stonework. Mortar or a putty-like filler is forced into the joint after the stone is set.
Underwriters Laboratories (UL)	an organization that classifies roof assemblies for their fire characteristics and wind uplift resistance.
Vapor Migration	the movement of water vapor from a region of high vapor pressure to a region of lower vapor pressure.
Vapor Retarder	a material designed to restrict the passage of water vapor through a roof or wall.
Vent	an opening designed to convey water vapor or other gas from inside a building or a building component to the atmosphere, thereby relieving vapor pressure.
Vermiculite	an aggregate used in lightweight insulating concrete, formed by the heating and consequent expansion of a micaceous mineral.
Water Cutoff	(See Cutoff.)
Waterproofing	treatment of a surface or structure to prevent the passage of water under hydrostatic pressure.
Wythe	a masonry wall, one masonry unit, a minimum of two inches thick.